Casey Stengel

Casey Stengel

HIS HALF-CENTURY IN BASEBALL

FRANK GRAHAM, Jr.

ILLUSTRATED

NEW YORK   The John Day Company

ILLUSTRATIONS

All following page 96

ACKNOWLEDGMENTS

The biography of Casey Stengel is a persistent serial which grows day by day in the pages of America's newspapers and magazines. His real biographers are the sports writers who have recorded his accomplishments and preserved the hundreds of anecdotes which have given Casey his unique place in the game of baseball. To all of the following go the author's grateful acknowledgments; the stories of each have been a source for material in this book: Red Smith, Arthur Daley, Dan Daniel, Tom Meany, John Lardner, Harold Rosenthal, Tommy Holmes, Roger Kahn, Jimmy Cannon, Milton Gross, Dan Parker, Jimmy Powers, John Carmichael, Bill Corum, Ed Linn, Ben Epstein, Milton Richman, John Drebinger, Jerry Mitchell, Joe Trimble, Harold Kaese, Arch Murray and Hugh Bradley. And, like all others who write about baseball, the author is heavily indebted to J. G. Taylor Spink and his invaluable publication, *The Sporting News*.

The author's debt to his father is greatest of all—for some of the material, of course, but even more for his encouragement and inspiration.

Casey Stengel

1.

"ROOTING FOR THE YANKEES," Jimmy Little, a television actor and Dodger fan, once told a group of friends, "is like rooting for U.S. Steel." Little's remark, widely quoted (and appropriated by needier wits) sums up the feelings of countless baseball buffs. Several generations have grown up looking upon the New York Yankees as a remorseless corporation which grinds down its opposition with an inevitability alien to our concept of sport. The team, its detractors claim, functions with cold efficiency and its individual players sparkle not with the animal vitality of the performer but with the soulless precision of the machine. Tension and excitement can be aroused only by combat among mortals, because they are subject to failure as well as success. The scent of mortality has seldom been detected about the Yankees.

On the whole, this viewpoint is unfair to the Yankees. It is true that their teams during the 1930's and most of the 40's, managed by the dour Joe McCarthy, came closer to this stereotyped image than the Yankees of old or their even more successful teams of today. McCarthy's Yankees, of whom Lou Gehrig with his stolid power and Joe DiMaggio with his almost lethargic grace were the popular symbols, beat their opponents brains out with a kind of passionless venom. They were seldom "good copy." Mc-Carthy became famous as "the push-button mana-ger," a term of derision applied to him by a rival be-cause, with his great collection of stars, he allegedly had only to sit back and push a button to get the home run or outstanding defensive play needed to win. Both Gehrig and DiMaggio finally became popular figures only by chance; poor Lou by contracting the rare disease which snuffed out his career and later his life, and DiMag by falling in love with Marilyn Mon-roe.

The Yankees of the Roaring Twenties were a differ-ent breed. It was Babe Ruth who loaned them a part of his own gargantuan personality and made them a nation's favorites. They were as bawdy and combative as any band of roustabouts attached to a wandering carnival. As much as they craved victory, they never let its pursuit blot out their idea of the good life. Ruth was more than their best player. He was their spiritual leader.

As the Babe was baseball's greatest figure in his day, so Casey Stengel, the manager of today's Yankees, has dominated the game since 1949. It is a tribute to his unique talents and personality that he, a non-player, overshadows not only his own super-stars but also such skillful or controversial players as Ted Williams, Willie Mays and Stan Musial. Casey, of course, has been a name, even a legend, in baseball for over forty-five years. He has contributed to that legend sometimes with alluvial imperceptibility, at other times with a mighty upheaval worthy of the gods. At 67, his peculiar legend is growing as never before.

10

He has done more than mold this great contemporary Yankee team from the clay—a superior brand of clay, to be sure—placed at his disposal. He has breathed life into it, and sent red blood coursing through its veins. To make it in his own image and likeness was beyond even his genius. After all, there could be only one Casey.

Superficially, Stengel's life story is like that of everyone else—a chronological procession of dates, incidents and achievements. But essentially it is a series of anecdotes, strung together by the thread of almost fifty years of wandering in baseball. His life has had a kind of fuzzy reality about it because Casey varies and embellishes the anecdotes on each retelling and the stories are further distorted as they are picked up and handed on by his listeners.

His achievements are real. They are in the baseball record books and baseball is one field in which the statistics never lose their charm for its followers. He was an outstanding outfielder for fourteen National League seasons. He was a World Series hero for the Giants in the twilight of his career, beating the Yankees twice with home runs in 1923. His batting average for three World Series (which included two earlier ones with Brooklyn) was a brilliant .393. And the eight American League pennants and six world championships he has won in only nine seasons with the Yankees form a record of consistent triumph unprecedented in the game's history. In the long run his record is surpassed only by John McGraw's ten pennants and Joe McCarthy's seven world titles.

To Stengel's unbounded annoyance those feats will

be forgotten long before the fans and writers stop retelling the story of how he doffed his cap to a jeering crowd and a sparrow flew out of it; how, when he was offered a better job while serving as president and manager of a minor league team and could not secure his release, he fired himself as manager and then resigned as president; how he conspired to drop a grapefruit on his manager, Wilbert Robinson, from an airplane; and how his failure to win with a miserable team in Boston so emphasized his clowning and sarcasm that, when he was run down by an automobile, a sports columnist suggested that the driver be awarded a plaque for having done the most for Boston baseball that season.

"Whenever I get introduced to people," Casey said before coming to the Yankees, "they say, 'Oh, you're the fella that hid the bird under his hat.'" Casey now fears it will be his fate to be remembered as a clown rather than as the astute chieftain who led the mighty Yankees to what begins to seem an endless string of pennants.

But never mind yesterday or tomorrow. Today Casey is a very lively and influential legend. Earning over $100,000 a year from the Yankees in salary and bonuses, he is the highest paid manager in baseball history. Those who insist he is a baseball genius need only point to his accomplishments to back up their belief. His superiority as a manager is chiefly a combination of imagination and the daring to order the moves that his imagination dictates. It follows that because these moves are imaginative they will be un-

12

orthodox, and it requires courage to follow consistently an unorthodox plan. That he has never lost his touch is the result of another of Casey's qualities—though he is getting old, he has always been open to new ideas. He has the wonderful capacity to learn from the young.

Stengel's life spans the whole history of modern baseball, linking the rough-and-tumble Baltimore Orioles of the 1890's with today's efficiency regime at the Yankee Stadium. He learned much of his baseball under John McGraw and Wilbert Robinson, two mainstays of the legendary Orioles, and, in this era of the lively ball and the big inning, he reaches back to pluck a trick from those old masters with a frequency that is disconcerting to his less-experienced contemporaries.

Some have put him down as a clown, and it is true that his rambling monologues and comic pantomimes have occasionally obscured for others his intense awareness of what is going on around him. In the midst of an apparently irrelevant anecdote he usually makes an important point to his players or a shrewd comment on the current game. More than one Yankee has learned the right way to make a play as he watched Casey cavort through a parody on the incompetent teams he managed in Brooklyn and Boston.

Casey, as manager of the Yankees, has done more than just carry on the Yankee tradition of victory. While he agrees with an earlier thinker who remarked that God is for the big battalions, he realizes that baseball fans are not. Today's public demands

13

that its heroes be human as well as triumphant, and Casey has added humanity to the many other imposing qualities of the Yankees. It is an ingredient in which he has never been deficient.

2.

YANKEE STADIUM is a three-tiered light beige concrete structure which stands on an eleven-acre plot of ground in New York City's Borough of the Bronx. Completed in 1923, it was first "The House That Ruth Built" and later "The Home of Champions." Stengel, who was named manager of the Yankees just two months after Ruth's death, has played a formidable role in keeping "The Home of Champions" exactly that. The Stadium serves as his place of business, a convenient lodge where he can meet his friends and as an enormous stage on which he can act out his many parts.

Here is a typical day with Casey at the Stadium. Not any particular one, but a day (or night) on which the Yankees are playing a contending team. A large crowd is in the stands and, most important of all, the dugout is swarming with the big-name sports writers and other important persons for whom Stengel reserves his finest performances.

He arrives early, usually well ahead of any of his players. It may be three hours or more before game time when he enters the Stadium through the glass door on 157th Street, walks through an air-conditioned corridor and into the Yankee clubhouse. This room, spacious, airy, clean and well-lighted, is the

15

Yankees' answer to the smelly little areas in which most professional athletes dress. It could pass for the clubhouse at one of our finer country clubs. Here each player has not just a locker, but a small cubicle in which to dress and to hang his clothes and equipment, large enough to sit in while he enjoys a smoke or the afternoon newspaper away from the hurly-burly around him.

At the end of this room, to the left, is Stengel's office and dressing room. It is furnished with a swivel chair, a roll top desk, and, more in keeping with the Stadium's modern décor, a green leather divan. On the desk is piled his mail, baseball record books, and an old trophy commemorating some dimly remembered event. The wall, which holds a number of photographs and cartoons of Stengel and a large picture of Babe Ruth, is dominated by an electric clock, brightly lighted like those found in drug stores and luncheonettes. In one corner of the room is a shower stall.

After a time the players begin to arrive. Yogi Berra, one of Stengel's favorites, arrives, hangs his jacket in his cell, and walks back toward the trainer's room. Stengel has heard a radio commercial earlier in which Yogi delivered a recorded plug for an ice cream company. "I heard you on the radio this morning," Casey says. "You were splendid."

Yogi lifts his eyebrows, grins, and continues into the trainer's room. Turning back to his office, Casey removes his gray silk sports shirt and sifts through the pile of mail on his desk. Most of the letters ask for his or his players' autographs, or criticize some recent piece of Stengelian strategy. As his coaches,

16

who dress in their own cells just outside Stengel's office, come in, Casey gives them their instructions. He also asks them to check on the physical condition of the ailing players. Jim Thomson, the Stadium superintendent, stops to discuss with him the condition of the playing field. Perhaps one of the players has told Casey there is a small hole in the outfield, or that the ground is too tightly packed on one side of the infield. "We inspect the field every day," Thomson will tell you, "but we can only *see* it. The players can *feel* it. They register their complaints with Casey, he passes them along to us, and we try to straighten things out."

Almost every day Casey talks with general manager George Weiss, either in the Yankees' downtown offices, not far from the hotel where Casey lives in New York, or in the manager's office at the Stadium. Then, when he has received a report on men too badly hobbled to play, he begins in his mind the tortuous line of reasoning which ultimately will bring forth the day's starting lineup. It will almost certainly differ from the one he used the day before.

A writer who wants to find Stengel comparatively alone for a few minutes has his best chance when Casey first comes on the field. His utility players are at batting practice and the horde of writers, photographers and celebrity-seekers has not yet arrived. Casey comes up from the tunnel which connects the clubhouse with the dugout and sits down on the padded bench, his sharp blue eyes already taking in every bit of action out on the field.

As a youth, Casey had a pleasantly homely face,

17

and, as so often happens, the earlier homeliness has been subjugated to the character stamped there by age. Incompetent ballplayers and years of defeat have seamed this face. Laughter and mimicry have rescued it from harshness. His features, which one moment have the flexibility of Rubber Face Gallagher's, can harden instantly into the mask of a Roman legion commander. Head-on, it is his immense ears (sails, Casey calls them) which one notices first. In profile, his nose, hawk-like but fleshy, is the most prominent landmark. When he stands, his body reflects a vitality which most of his players, forty years younger, cannot approach. He is five feet, ten inches tall, but, because of his stocky build and the odd, curled-over walk the years have given him, he appears several inches shorter. He walks, someone has said, like a man whose vest is buttoned to his pants.

Now his audience begins to arrive, coming into the dugout one by one and pointing straight for Casey like pigeons in the park converging on a man with a bag of popcorn. He sits at the end of the dugout, one leg cocked up on the bench, bracing himself on an extended arm as he leans back. From time to time he pulls off his cap, revealing his unruly gray hair, and, pointing with the visor, indicates a player on the field. Then he slaps the cap on his knee and jams it back, cockeyed this time, on his head. Kenny Smith, the tiny baseball writer of *The Daily Mirror,* comes up.

"I'm pitching my man Shantz for you today, Smitty," Casey says in his gravel voice. "He's just your height, so I want you to write the best article that's gonna be done about him."

18

As the writers crowd around him, some scribbling notes, others merely enjoying the show, Casey hurls himself into a monologue. These monologues are only partly dependent upon words. He makes his most dramatic points with a shrug, a wink, a sudden lunge or a hideous facial expression. The words, more or less intelligible, serve as incidental music—a kind of phraseless melody. While he dwells almost exclusively on baseball, he ranges with bewildering rapidity over the whole course of his experience. An anecdote, apparently sailing in one direction, suddenly veers in quite another and the listener whose ears are not attuned to Stengelese is soon as hopelessly lost as a mariner without charts and compass.

The story is told of the writer who left his companions in the press box to visit the Yankee dugout. "Find out who's pitching for the Yankees tomorrow," one of the others called after him. Arriving in the dugout, he walked up to Casey and asked him about the next day's pitcher. Casey, remarking that the man he had in mind had an aching shoulder, was suddenly reminded of the time that Christy Mathewson came down with a similar ailment in 1912. From there his conversation touched on other old-time pitchers, wandered to John McGraw, and finally ended with a partially intelligible anecdote of Casey's days as an outfielder with the Dodgers. The writer, mildly shell-shocked, stumbled back to the press box.

"Did you find out who's pitching tomorrow?" a colleague asked him.

The writer shrugged. "As nearly as I can make out," he said, "it's going to be Christy Mathewson."

It's a nice story, but the writer undoubtedly came away with Casey's pitcher for the following day, too. The pre-game audiences with Stengel are informative, as well as amusing. A question from one of the writers about the team, particularly if the Yankees are experiencing stormy days, invariably brings forth a detailed analysis of its condition.

"My men did very good work on the road," Casey says, settling back, his arms folded. "We been winning on the road, but we can't win at home. The ground's too smooth here, I guess. My shortstop missed the ball the other day and we lost a game. One fella I see out there I think is dreaming because even when he gets the ball he don't seem to have his mind on what he's doing, and another fella looks as though he believes he's never going to get another hit again and they're getting him out on low balls although I remember when if you threw him a low ball he wouldn't ground it but he'd hit it—whisst!—into the grandstands. And then when we *are* getting some hits we aren't getting them when we have somebody on the bases. It's very aggravating. But maybe it's better to see them left there than not getting them on at all. If they keep getting on you got to figure one of these days they'll be getting home. Or it could be one of these years, you know."

Restless now, he gets up and paces the dugout. Then he chins himself once on the dugout roof and sits down again. "When we were in Detroit last week a woman walked up to me in the hotel and asked me if I was the manager. Now how did she know I was

20

the manager? Because of the worried look on my face, that's how."

One of the writers asks him about the injuries the Yankees have had. Casey rubs his chin and looks up at the dugout roof.

"Bauer's hurt," he says. "He might not play today."

"What's wrong with him?"

"I don't know. I only went to college for eight hours and I hear it takes eight years to get a medical degree." Having delivered this morsel of fiction, the man who attended Western Dental College for two years wags his head and goes on. "The way things are going with us right now our fellas are getting hurt on their days off. They don't even have to come to the ball park to do it, which as you can see is a great improvement over the old days. Tuesday when we're going to play a night game I'm out here at three o'clock in the afternoon but at seven o'clock I don't know what my lineup is going to be. One fella I think is going to play says to me then, 'I can't play tonight. My arm still hurts, the same as it did on Sunday.'

" 'Why didn't you put it in the whirlpool bath like I told you?' I ask him.

" 'I was going to,' he tells me, 'but when I got here at six o'clock there are six or eight other fellas waiting for the whirlpool.'

" 'Well,' I says, 'I thought you worked here like I do. I was here at three o'clock.' He must have paid attention, because he was out here early today and got his arm in the whirlpool bath and now he tells me he's ready to play."

21

There is a pause, rather than a break, in Casey's monologue as he peers out at the batting cage.

"Look at that fella up there," he says, pointing to a Yankee who has just stepped into the cage for his practice swings. "He's big and strong and he can hit that fast ball. What he should do now is ask the pitcher to throw him some curves and soft stuff. But, no, he hits the fast ball best and so that's all he wants to see. He'll be up there in a game with two strikes on him and a pitcher like Pierce will break one off on him down here and then he will look at the umpire and ask him, 'What's that?' And the umpire will tell him, 'You're out.'

"The reason is that these young fellas don't see curve balls like that in the minor leagues and when they get to see them up here they're astonished. Just astonished."

Casey watches a hitter in the cage skip away from a ball thrown down around his ankles. He looks up at one of the writers and winks. "I've seen the time when it wouldn't do a club no harm if a fella let the ball hit him on the ankle and then limped down to first base. How bad is it going to hurt you if you get hit in the leg with the ball? You'd think they shot it at you out of a cannon the way these fellas jump away from it. Did you ever hear of a man getting his foot amputated because he was hit with a baseball?"

Here he jumps to his feet and hobbles the length of the dugout, like an old man on a cane. "Oh, doctor!" he yells toward the batting cage. "Come cut off my foot, I just got hit by a baseball! Oh, doctor, come cut off my foot! Oh, please, doctor, it hurts so

22

bad." The players turn to stare for a moment at the jig Stengel is performing in the dugout, then turn away again as if the sight were one they see every day.

Berra is crouched on the top step of the dugout, listening to him. Casey, sitting down again and crossing his legs, points to his catcher, who has been out of the lineup with an injury. "Now there's a sad case, that Berra. Trying to get into the $125,000 a year class —and now he'll never make it because he's missed a couple of games this season. He don't want to sit down because he loves to talk to them other hitters, too, and he's afraid if he don't play he'll miss all that gossip. But anyway it'll give some of my other catchers a chance to play before their equipment goes out of style."

Casey, whose oil wells and real estate investments have long since relieved him of dependence upon baseball for a living, takes an almost childish delight in poking fun at his bosses. If he sees Weiss in the stands taking notes, he mimics him, holding an imaginary notebook on his knee and scribbling furiously. Somebody asks him about owner Dan Topping, who has been ill.

"He's got ulcers," Casey says sadly. "This race has been too close for him, and he worries. I guess I'll have to win every game or else I'll get fired. But I've got it pretty soft because Yogi here is always in good with the bosses. Ain't that right, Yogi? You'll put in a good word for me, won't you, Yogi?"

The Yankees, having finished their batting practice, go back to the clubhouse to smoke and change their shirts. Casey stays behind in the dugout. While continuing his monologue, he carefully watches the visiting players take their swings. If he notices that one of them has changed his stance or is hitting to the opposite field more often, he will mention it to his pitcher before the game. It may mean nothing, it may mean the difference between a game won and a game lost.

Now the stands are filling up. A writer or a friend of a friend may bring into the dugout an excited boy to shake hands with Casey and meet some of the players. Casey is genuinely fond of children and his face lights up when one is brought over to him. Writer Ed Linn recalls the day when a boy, his face shining, was escorted into the dugout, hesitantly extending his scorecard for an autograph. "I'm Jimmy McPherson. I wrote you from Shreveport and—"

Casey, of course, has never heard of the boy, but he does not have to be prompted. "So *you're* Jimmy McPherson," he says, taking the scorecard from him and shaking his hand. "Sure, I got your letter. I been wondering what was keeping you. That was a very nice letter." And then, making a shrewd guess, "You said your father was bringing you here, right?"

The boy, overwhelmed, can only gulp and grin, and Casey takes him around, introducing him to the players in the dugout and commenting on the recent fortunes of the Yankees. "This here is Mickey Mantle. He thinks he's gotta imitate Stan Musial. Everybody else is imitating Mantle, and he's gotta imitate Musial."

The boy is now a Yankee fan for life.

It is nearing game time and Casey retires from the

24

dugout for a hasty lunch. He eats in the press club under the stands, being served at the bar there with the specialty of the day, perhaps a sandwich, perhaps creamed fish. Here, too, the writers crowd around him and he delivers a discourse on whatever subject has been brought up. Finishing his lunch, he wipes his mouth with a paper napkin, puts on his cap and says, "If that's all, gentlemen, I think I'll get out on the field. I see by the papers I'm supposed to play a ball game with the White Sox."

The demands of maneuvering the Yankees to victory do not interfere with Stengel's dramatic performance. He is always on stage. Watching him in the dugout as he paces up and down, flaps his long arms, calls to his players on the field, or slumps in dejection on the bench, is as much a part of attending a Yankee game as keeping track of the hits and runs. The photographer or television cameraman who does not poke his lens into the dugout occasionally to pick up Casey, the number "37" prominent on the back of his uniform, is not thoroughly covering the game.

He ceaselessly prowls back and forth, bellowing insults at the opposition or exhortations to his own men, sometimes bouncing to the top of the steps to shout a protest at an offending umpire and then quickly ducking back down behind his own proscenium, the edge of the dugout. As he prowls he has been heard to sing snatches of half-forgotten ditties. A few years ago he made up derisive couplets to sing to the opposition in his gravel-throated voice, ending each with a refrain that went, "Tra, la, la, la, la! Tra, la, la, la, la!"

25

Having worked so long for success, he knows no worse terror than seeing victory slip through his fingers. He is at his worst, is most jittery, when the Yankees are ahead. Then he treads the dugout floor like a caged animal and the spectators can almost hear him as he snarls to his players, "Don't let 'em up! Don't let 'em up!" He is quick to pull out a pitcher who appears to be tiring. If his team is behind as he bounces up the dugout steps, head thrust forward and half running toward the mound, his detractors among the crowd wait for him. Then, placing all the blame for the Yankees' poor showing on the manager, they shower him with abuse, just as certain Chinese peasants beat their little stone rain gods in times of drought.

The game over, he is once again surrounded by the writers, this time in his office under the stands. His cap and shoes off, his uniform shirt unbuttoned, he reclines on the leather couch while the reporters ask him questions about the game. If he has lost, he is tired but hopeful. If he has won, he is tired and apprehensive.

"Did you feel that winning this one takes some of the heat off you?" a writer asks.

"The heat," Casey says, running a hand through his hair, "is never off until you win the last game of the Series."

It is a lesson painfully learned through almost fifty years in professional baseball.

3.

MAYSVILLE IS a small city on the Ohio River in northern Kentucky. Daniel Boone once operated a tavern there, and Ulysses S. Grant spent some time in this seat of Mason County, attending not Boone's tavern but a local school. By the late summer of 1910 the tavern and the school had been replaced by, among other landmarks, a county insane asylum and, just across the road, a field on which the local team in the Blue Grass Baseball League played its games. The citizens of Maysville who visited the ball park were treated to a spectacle uncommon even in a town blessed by such an historic past. One of the out-fielders was a bandy-legged youth with blond hair, freckles, and a pair of large ears which would have distinguished him at a distance if his conduct on the field had not already set him apart from his team-mates. He had a loud voice and a kind of clumsy skill, and he played the game with the ferocious energy which only the very young can squander on hot, sleepy afternoons.

It was in pre-game practice that he was most often an object of the fans' curiosity. When a fly ball was hit to him he would settle under it, make the catch, and then go through an extraordinary series of ac-tions. He would throw the ball back to the infield, and toss his glove in the opposite direction. Then he would set his bandy legs in motion and race across the outfield grass in pursuit of the glove. When he came to within a few strides of it he would launch into a vigorous slide as if the battered leather glove were home plate and he carried the winning run. On the Maysville bench one of the veteran players once thoughtfully shook his head and said to a teammate seated next to him: "It's only a matter of time before that Stengel will be leaving us."

"You mean he's going up to the majors?" asked the other player.

"No," said the veteran, pointing to the nearby asylum, "over there."

Even at this early date, there was method in Casey Stengel's madness. "I was getting a jump on those guys who were wasting time sitting around," he said years afterward. "You see, I practiced catching, throwing, running and sliding all at once."

Having applied himself with such diligence to his chosen profession, Stengel had moved from the sand-lots of Kansas City to the ball park at Maysville in a remarkably short time. He was to move from there to the big leagues almost as rapidly. The clown in Casey had vied right from the beginning with that ambitious cunning which even now drives him to get the jump on his rivals and, once out in front, stay there. In the years to come his reputation as a clown was sometimes to be a burden, but in the main these two qualities would work together to bring him a fame and success that few other men in sports have enjoyed. "Being a clown wasn't safe in the minors," Stengel once

28

said. "Some of them bush-league managers could hit you with a bat at fifty feet." But corporal punishment could not have stopped Casey from playing the fool, any more than it kept Huck Finn from playing hookey.

There is much about any legend, living or dead, that is obscure, and so it has been with Stengel. The stories about him have become twisted over the years and pranks have been laid at his door as indiscriminately as other people's epigrams were attributed to Oscar Wilde. Even the date of his birth given in most record books (1891) misses the mark by a full year. July 30, 1890, is the date now accepted by most students of this particular legend, for Charles Dillon Stengel, when he enrolled in high school on January 29, 1906, wrote that he was "15½ years." As he was younger then, it is felt that he may have been more truthful about his age, or, at least, that his memory was better. He was born on Agnes Avenue in the middle-class residential section of northeast Kansas City, Missouri.

Casey's mother, the former Jennie Gordon, was Irish, and his father, Louis, was German. When asked about his father's occupation, he has always replied that he operated a "sprinkler wagon." The truth is far more prosaic. The elder Stengel was a businessman who worked for the Joseph Stiebel Insurance Co. To-day's insurance companies dabble in real estate and other important matters, but in those days they evidently did not set their sights so high. Joseph Stiebel, Insurance, held contracts with the city for sprinkling the downtown streets. Many of the roads leading to the shopping section of Kansas City were unpaved, and great gobs of mud were spread in front of the stores by passing horses and wagons. It was one of Louis Stengel's jobs with the insurance firm to obtain and renew sprinkling contracts with the city. The sprinklers, older residents of Kansas City point out, were not the ideal solution to the problem. They could keep down the dust in front of the stores, but they could not eradicate the mud and dirt from the sidewalks.

Louis sired three young Stengels, a boy, Grant, a girl, Louise, and Charles. Perhaps because of his German ancestry, perhaps because he was blond, blue-eyed, and moderately plump, young Charles came to be called "Dutch" in the days when he was reluctantly pursuing his studies at Woodland and Garfield grade schools and playing baseball on the vacant lots along Agnes Avenue. The Stengel brothers, according to Casey, did occasionally work on the sprinkling wagons. "I wasn't much good at sprinklin', though," is how he sums up that phase of his life, and so one profession was stricken from the field of opportunities that lay before him.

The future broadened considerably for young Dutch while he was attending Kansas City's Central High School. He played basketball and football there and was elected captain of the football team during his senior year, 1909. Charles Dillon Stengel was a leader even then. In the spring he served as a left-handed second and third baseman on the baseball team, before turning to pitching. The school's 1910 year book, *The Centralian,* mentions only Stengel in a review of its baseball season:

"The baseball team this year was strong in almost every way, with the feature the hurling of Stengel."

For the first time he learned that he could put his talents as a baseball player to use. Harzfeld's, a prominent downtown women's store, had a ball club in the merchants' league. Louis Stengel was a business acquaintance of the store's owner, Sieg Harzfeld, and bragged to him of the pitching prowess of his son. Harzfeld, in need of a pitcher, took Dutch on; he was paid $1.50 a game, the same "contract" awarded to each of the Harzfeld players. When Casey and his wife, Edna, returned to Kansas City with the Yankees in the spring of 1955, Edna received a bottle of French perfume from the Harzfeld store. Attached to it was a note recalling that Sieg Harzfeld had been Casey's first employer in baseball.

Like other young bucks of his day, Dutch frequented the local pool hall, but his favorite after-dark pastime was sitting in the old Olympia Theater where he could watch the vaudeville troupers who visited Kansas City. Because of his own gift for mimicry he was fascinated by the comedians, and he spent many hours in the darkened theater laughing at the comics and absorbing small gestures and remarks that he could add to his own abundant natural fund.

Sitting in the theater, the idea, pleasant but vague, passed through Stengel's active mind that he might put his comic talents to work, as he had already done with his baseball talents, and earn his living in vaude-

31

ville. He was sure he was a better clown than many of the troupers he had paid to see. In the cold light of day, however, a stronger idea was taking hold of him. The professions, with their attendant security and dignity, appealed to this practical young man, and he began to think that dentistry might be a pleasant career. Western Dental College was nearby, and his limited experience with Harzfeld's had convinced him there was enough money to be earned pitching a baseball to pay for his instruments and tuition.

In the spring of 1910, while waiting to graduate from Central High, he reported for a tryout with the Kansas City Blues. Their training camp was at nearby Excelsior Springs, Missouri, where another celebrated American, Jesse James, had grown up. Young Dutch Stengel was eager to impress the Blues' manager, Danny Shay, with his skill as a southpaw pitcher, but the Blues' regulars eyed his pitches as hungrily as the James boys had looked on heavily laden trains. After several days of harsh treatment at the hands of the hitters, Stengel was dispatched to the outfield on the theory that he couldn't be any worse out there. He could catch fly balls all right, but the fences, as they do any young man who has played only in open lots, gave him trouble. Having set himself to field a ball which was bouncing off the fence, he was invariably fooled by the sharp carom. "Play the angles!" Shay shouted at him one day. "Learn to play the angles!"

"If you want somebody to play the angles," Stengel growled, "why don't you hire a pool player?"

The next day Dutch was on his way home.

When he had lined up his courses for the fall at

Western Dental College, he joined the Kankakee team in the Northern Association, a league which soon folded so completely that not even *The Sporting News* has been able to find any trace of his record there. By July he had arrived in Maysville, where he soon had both his teammates and the neighboring inmates shaking their heads, but he failed to leave a lasting impression with enemy pitchers. He finished the season with the dismal batting average of .223. He had, however, earned $150 a month there, enough to get him started in dental school. His batting average would seem to imply that Dutch had chosen the proper career.

The following year he played at Aurora, Illinois, in the Illinois-Wisconsin League, where he began to discover that hitting a baseball wasn't any tougher than making people laugh and certainly wasn't as hard as pulling other people's teeth. He batted .352 to lead the league and, though he did not realize it at the time, he had crossed his own particular Rubicon. He had come to the attention of the Brooklyn Baseball Club in a more haphazard manner than his performance that year might have merited. The Dodgers had a scout in those days whose name was Larry Sutton. He roamed the entire country looking for ballplayers, and in the course of his travels he discovered some of the greatest players ever to play for Brooklyn, among them Dazzy Vance—and Casey Stengel.

"I was in Chicago in the summer of 1911," Sutton recalled years later, "and I didn't know where to go from there. I walked down to the railroad station and looked at the signs and one of them said that a train was going to Aurora. So I bought a ticket on it because I'd heard there was some minor league up that way and I figured maybe I'd see somebody I liked. When I got to the ball park there I saw this kid Stengel and he had a good day. Better than that, he had blond hair and freckles, and a kid with that combination is always a fighter."

That Stengel belonged to the Dodgers did not mean he was yet a genuine big-leaguer. The Dodgers had drafted him for $300 from the Aurora club and, after originally assigning his contract to Toronto, finally ordered him to report the following spring to the training camp of the Montgomery, Alabama, team. Stengel, who was now the property of a major league team, however frail he considered the link that bound him to it, had already picked up something all his own in his brief wanderings through the minors. That was the nickname he still bears—"Casey." Even the name he has made famous in baseball is of no very certain origin. It is generally assumed that it was applied to him because he came from Kansas City—K.C.— but Stengel himself isn't sure. "The poem 'Casey At The Bat' was popular in them days," he once told a writer, "and the name Casey was hung on a lot of players. Maybe that's how it started."

Meanwhile, this practical young man was taking nothing for granted as he waited to report to Pensacola, Florida, where the Montgomery team had its training camp. That winter, fortified by the earnings of a full season of baseball, he went back to his pliers and drills at Western Dental. (It has been written that

34

Casey attended a "correspondence school," but this is not so. Western Dental was a highly reputable institution which later merged with Kansas City Dental College to become Kansas City Western Dental, and this in turn only a few years ago became a part of the University of Kansas City.) There was a difference, though, in his attitude. He went at his studies with perhaps a shade less enthusiasm than he had brought to them a year before. It wasn't merely that his mind was already on spring training at Pensacola, or even on Washington Park, where the Dodgers then played their games. Casey was beginning to suspect that, whether or not he was a ballplayer, he surely wasn't a dentist.

"I was pretty good at inlays," he says, "but I couldn't measure up at making caps. I still gotta shudder when I see an old tin can. It reminds me of some of my work. But I guess the beginning of the end was when I tried to pull a tooth. This was in the clinic and the professor gave me the job of demonstrating on some poor fella who walked in off the street. You didn't have to pay to have a tooth pulled at the school. This fella had a toothache but I don't think he had any money or he never would have let us get our hands on him. Well, it turned out he was very tall and I didn't set the chair low enough for him. When I put the clamp on him he came right up out of the chair and I'm reaching higher and higher and pretty soon I'm at the top of my reach like I'm trying for a high line drive and we still hadn't settled who was going to have the tooth, him or me. I finally wrestled him out of it, but it was no fun for either of us."

And so, to the relief of Kansas City's cavity-ridden paupers, spring came at last and Casey packed his glove and spikes and set out for Pensacola. He was beginning to feel his oats now, both as a ballplayer and as a clown. Before an exhibition game that spring he was shagging flies in the outfield when he felt underfoot a manhole cover partly hidden in the grass. Prying it up, he peeked inside and saw the hole was but a few feet deep and contained only a coiled hose. When the game started Casey trotted out to his position in left field. Later, after the first batter had lifted a fly ball in that direction, the crowd (and Casey's teammates) were startled to discover that Montgomery's leftfielder had apparently evaporated.

"I jumped down in the hole when I went out there," Casey says, "and of course nobody was watching what the leftfielder was doing. I lifted up the lid just far enough so I could see where the ball was hit and when it came my way I stood up holding this lid over my head like a shield. The crowd let out a gasp I could hear all the way out in left field. I was going to let the ball hit the lid and bounce up in the air and then I'd catch it on the way down again. But the lid was heavier than I figured. I couldn't get it all the way up there and I was staggering around under the load and I was sure the ball was going to hit me on the head. At the last second I reached out with one hand and grabbed it. My manager was pretty mad about it, but the crowd loved it and of course I caught the ball so that helped some."

By September the brash young man who had startled the crowd in Pensacola was playing baseball, and his tricks, in Brooklyn. The Dodgers, struggling through a bleak season in which they were destined to finish seventh, cast about for some outfield help and finally settled on Stengel. He was batting .290 at Montgomery and was the best rookie then available. While at Montgomery, Casey had been befriended by Kid Elberfeld, a veteran shortstop with thirteen big league seasons behind him. The excited young man was packing for his trip to Brooklyn when Elberfeld looked in on him to say goodbye. The older man took a horror-stricken look at Casey's suitcase—a cardboard valise which was already beginning to disintegrate.

"That's okay in good weather," Elberfeld told him, "but what'll happen if you get caught in the rain? You'll be walking along holding nothing but a handle. If you're going to the big leagues, buy yourself a decent suitcase."

"A good suitcase costs twenty bucks," Stengel reminded him. "I been playing ball to get enough money to go back to school and I can't save anything if I walk around laying out twenty bucks for suitcases."

"Forget about school," Elberfeld said. "You're going to the big leagues and you ain't going back to school. You're a ballplayer now."

Casey realized he was right. He arrived in New York a few days later with a new suitcase and ninety-five dollars in his pocket, as bewildered as any young man who has ever come to the big city to earn his fortune. He spent his first night in the Longacre Hotel on West Forty-Seventh Street and, though tempted by the nearby lights of Broadway, was reluctant to venture out of his room. To step from the hotel into the swirling mass of people on the sidewalks seemed as foolhardy as plunging into a roaring torrent; he would certainly be swept away. He soon gathered the courage to leave the hotel, but his foray was brief and he was quickly back in the safety of his tiny room, excited and somewhat alarmed.

An even greater adventure lay before him. The next morning, September 12, 1912, he was up early and on his way across the East River to Brooklyn. With the aid of elevated and street car rides, and numerous directions from the friendly natives, he arrived at Washington Park. The gatekeeper, seeing a strange face, was suspicious at first, but Casey soon convinced him he was the Dodgers' new outfielder and was let in. As Casey was let into the park, the gatekeeper said, "The clubhouse is down there—and you'd better be good."

When he walked in the Brooklyn players were shooting craps in front of a cluster of old lockers. No one glanced up at the newcomer except Zack Wheat, one of the greatest players the Dodgers have ever had. He introduced Casey around and the others, sensing they had in hand a bird ready for plucking, welcomed him with a cordiality seldom extended to rookies. Twenty of his precious dollars had passed into other hands when he heard a sharp voice behind him. "Are you a ballplayer or a crapshooter, kid?"

Casey looked up into the face of the Dodgers' manager, Bill Dahlen. He affirmed that he was a ballplayer.

"Then suit up and get out on the field while you've still got carfare left."

It was an unsettling beginning for a day which was to turn out so happily for the Dodgers' newest player. Dahlen told Stengel he was to start in center field. There wasn't much of a crowd in the stands, for it was late in the season and the Dodgers were deep in the second division. But across the street, beyond the outfield wall, rose the Ginney Flats, on whose network of fire escapes the residents gathered to watch their heroes. Those who had extra space there rented it to neighbors at ten cents a head. By game time the citizens of South Brooklyn were assembling at their vantage points and enterprising saloon keepers were selling growlers of beer to the fans perched above them, the fans hoisting the growlers from the street on ropes supplied by the publicans. They were enthusiastic, if rowdy, spectators, and while they usually defended their heroes with loud words, and occasionally with fists, a bad play by a Dodger could quickly alter their good spirits. They alternately hurled cheers and maledictions at their favorites, and they bombarded enemy outfielders with spears fashioned from umbrella ribs. In Stengel they found a player who could trade greetings and insults with them on even terms, and on occasion shout them down.

The gatekeeper, admitting Stengel to Washington Park, had reminded him that he had "better be good." The harsh cries of the mob looking down from the sub-Olympian heights of the Ginney Flats prompted Casey to reflect that the gatekeeper should have added

"—and be quick about it." They were an impatient panel of critics. Always alert to a favorable opportunity, Casey rose to the occasion with a performance unusual even in that borough where the spectacular is commonplace. Facing Pittsburgh's Claude Hendrix, one of the league's better pitchers, he hammered out four straight hits and twice stole second base. On Casey's last trip to the plate, with a lefthander now pitching for the Pirates, Pittsburgh manager Fred Clarke shouted from the dugout: "Okay, busher, let's see you cross over."

Casey, who had never batted righthanded, cockily stepped across the plate and assumed a righthanded stance. Perhaps unnerved by this brash young man (or rattled by the menace of an accurately aimed umbrella rib), the Pittsburgh lefty walked Stengel on four pitches.

The fans loved this rookie who had so enlivened what otherwise would have been an unexciting game. Stengel not only looked like a good ballplayer, a rare enough commodity in Brooklyn then, but he had color and aggressiveness, both of which the citizens of that borough have always prized in their heroes. "The next day the papers said I looked like the new Ty Cobb," he said afterward, "but pretty soon they found out I was nothing but the old Casey Stengel."

That, to be sure, was no mean discovery. Casey was now in the big leagues, and it would be thirteen years before they could get him out again. Meanwhile he was to find that every game would not be as easy as his first. He got one lesson a couple of days later when the Cubs came to Brooklyn. He was on first base and

40

was flashed the sign to steal. The Cub catcher fired the ball down to second base and Johnny Evers, a fierce little competitor, took the throw in plenty of time to tag Casey. Never giving up on the play, the rookie outfielder slid hard into Evers in an unsuccessful try to knock the ball from his grasp. "The next time you try that, you busher," Evers growled, "I'll stick the ball down your throat."

Casey glared at him. "That's the way I slid in the bushes, and that's the way I'm going to slide up here. My name is Stengel, Evers. Take a good look at me. I'm going to be around for a long time."

Evers fumed in anger. Rookies usually got their lumps right from the start, absorbed them as best they could, and seldom talked back. This busher was an exception, and Johnny did not forget him. Before a game the following spring, after Evers had been appointed manager of the Cubs, he passed the Brooklyn dugout where he accepted the congratulations of some of the older Dodgers. Stengel sat silently in a corner.

"What's the matter, Stengel?" Evers called to him. "Don't you want to wish me luck?"

Casey's homely face broke into a grin. "Sure I do, John. I just wanted to see if you remembered me."

Despite the early and rather explosive evidence that Stengel was utterly without fear, the league's pitchers were determined to find out for themselves. No rookie was going to hit consistently against them without first proving that he could dodge a pitch thrown at his head and come up out of the dirt to take a good cut at the next one. Casey recently recalled those days. "Nowadays when a pitch comes a little close to a fella he walks back to the dugout with a funny look on his face and says, 'You know, I think that pitcher was throwing at me.' When I joined the Dodgers I *knew* they was throwing at me. The first month I was in the league I spent three weeks lying on my back at the plate."

In the brief intervals during which he remained upright, Casey did some effective swinging. He batted .316 in the seventeen games he played that season and even clouted a home run, a feat he had not been able to accomplish in Maysville, Aurora or Montgomery. It was a good beginning.

The next couple of years were to bring important changes in Brooklyn, but Casey continued to establish himself as one of the most popular players who had ever worn a Dodger uniform. When the 1913 season opened the team moved into a new home— Ebbets Field, which had been completed during the winter and named for the president of the Dodgers. The following year Dahlen was dismissed as manager and replaced by Wilbert Robinson, a stout, tobacco-chewing veteran of the baseball wars who had played with John McGraw on the Baltimore Orioles back in the Nineties. "Uncle" Robbie could swear and growl with the best of them in an age when managers, considering it a grievous flaw in the structure of baseball that they were not allowed to beat their charges with sticks, made up for it in part with their savage tongues. But Robbie had a kindly heart and his players bowed to his whims as they would to those of an eccentric maiden aunt. He was a fitting leader for the "daffiness boys" who would people Brooklyn teams in the years to come.

Having abandoned his studies at Western Dental College, Casey now threw himself into the task of developing his baseball skills. Ebbets Field had a concrete wall in right field, a novelty in the game then, and Casey's agile mind quickly found a way to utilize it. "I used to come out to the park early," he once recalled, "and borrow three practice balls from Dan Comerford, our clubhouse man. They was so fuzzy they looked like they was wrapped in fur coats. Then I'd take them out and throw them up against the wall so I could watch how they'd come off. That way I got to know the angles." He had learned that a knowledge of angles is not necessarily restricted to pool players.

Casey had another weakness that he was determined to overcome. He went to Nap Rucker, the Dodgers' great lefthander, for help. "I couldn't hit a spitball to save my life," Casey said. "I used to bat at them like a guy chopping wood. Rucker took me out in the mornings. He wasn't a spitball pitcher but he had a curve that behaved like one. He worked with me for a long while and I finally got to swing at that low pitch like a golfer. I began to learn to hit the spitball and that kept me in the league."

He made few mistakes on the field, but Uncle Robbie let him know about those few. Once he almost lost a fly ball in a tight game and afterward Robinson fired a sarcastic volley at him: "If I watch you staggering around under them fly balls long enough I'll get a heart attack."

43

Stengel glared at Robbie for a moment, then turned to hang his shirt in his locker.

"Oh, well," Robbie said, "with legs and a behind like that you shouldn't be a ballplayer. You should be a—"

Stengel turned quickly. "I should be a what?"

Robbie shook his head. "I was just trying to think. But I give up."

Even Stengel joined in the laughter that followed.

Devoted as he was to the game, baseball could never be a grinding routine for Stengel. There were good times and a thousand laughs. One of Casey's memories of those days with the Dodgers is of a trip to Jersey City for an exhibition game. As an added attraction the management scheduled a pre-game contest in which a greased pig was turned loose in the outfield and a cash prize was awarded the player who caught it. Stengel, who has never bought a pig in a poke, was not going to let this one get away from him—not with fifty dollars riding on it. "I caught the pig and got the fifty bucks, which I needed. But I got enough grease on me to send a ship down the ways. I had to stand in the outfield between innings because I smelled so bad the other players wouldn't let me sit on the bench."

Casey's mother, who was very proud of her famous son, made a trip to Brooklyn once (and only once) to see him play. Not being familiar with the species of fan which inhabits that lusty borough, she was terribly upset when the crowd abused Casey for a bad play he had made in the field. "Come on, Louise," she said to her daughter as she got up from her seat.

44

"I think we'd better go home. I can't listen to any more of this."

Later that evening Casey explained to his mother that all Brooklyn fans shouted things like that and it meant only that they were fond of him. Mrs. Stengel thought it a queer means of expressing their affection, and from that time on she followed her son's exploits through the less harrowing medium of the sports pages.

Casey had arrived in Brooklyn at a happy moment. The Dodgers' fortunes were on the rise and, though they had yet to win a pennant in what the game's historians like to call "modern times" (i.e., this century), they were beginning to flex their muscles. By 1916 Robbie and Ebbets had put together a sound ball club and there was the feeling in Brooklyn that "next year" had arrived. It was a confident and determined band of players that reported to the Dodgers' camp at Daytona Beach in the spring. And, with Stengel around, there was sure to be some clowning, too. One day Robbie and a group of his players were at the beach when Ruth Law, a pretty young aviatrix, flew over in a plane with a sporting goods salesman who dropped a number of golf balls onto the sand as a publicity stunt. Uncle Robbie, an old Baltimore Oriole, was not impressed by the speed with which the golf balls came down, nor by the depth to which they buried themselves in the sand.

"If somebody threw a baseball out of a plane," he announced to his players, "I bet I could catch it."

The players snickered, but Robbie grew more enthusiastic. "Maybe not from as high as that plane was, but let somebody drop a ball to me from about four hundred feet and I'll catch it."

"If the ball hit you on the head it would smash your skull," laughed one of the players.

Robbie now grew indignant. "I never got hit on the head with a baseball, and I wouldn't get hit on the head with one even if it was dropped from that plane. You wait and see."

And so the experiment was put into operation and a plan was duly hatched. Though Casey later denied it was his plot, neither Robbie nor anyone else took the denial seriously. The following day a curious crowd gathered on the beach to watch this unprecedented spectacle. Robbie put on a catcher's mitt and waited as Miss Law circled overhead and then made her run on the beach. In the plane with her was the Dodger trainer, Frank Kelly, who had been designated bombardier for the flight. He was armed, not with a baseball, but with a large, juicy Florida grapefruit.

As the plane roared overhead, Robbie stretched out his arms and searched the sky for the ball. He saw something drop from the plane and began to circle under it. Bracing himself in the sand, he waited for the object as it grew in a second from the size of a pea to a great round yellow ball which blotted out the sky and, hurtling through his hands, seemed to explode in his face.

The impact of the grapefruit smashing into his chest knocked him flat on his back and he lay in the sand, covered with juice. His eyes closed and his fists

46

clenched, he began to cry: "I'm killed! I'm covered with blood! I'm blind! Somebody help me!"

So deep was he in what he thought were his death throes that he didn't hear the roar of laughter around him. In a moment he opened his eyes, slowly looked about, finally summoned the courage to peek down at his chest and saw that he was covered, not with his own life's blood, but with the juice and pulp of a badly squashed grapefruit. He leaped to his feet and the crowd scattered in the wake of some of the most blistering language ever to fill the Dixie air. He was mortified. For a time Stengel's job seemed in jeopardy, but it was not Robbie's nature to hold a grudge for what even he had to admit was a pretty good joke. To the day when he died, though, he insisted that had it been a baseball he would have held it.

The events of the 1916 season helped Uncle Robbie to forget the grapefruit. The Dodgers got off in front, threw back their main contenders and then withstood a furious drive by the Giants, who won twenty-six straight games during September, to win the league pennant. Casey batted .279 during the season, then, ever the opportunist, hit .364 in the World Series. His efforts there were not enough, however, and the Dodgers fell before the Red Sox in five games. It is one of Casey's fondest memories that he played on Brooklyn's first pennant-winning team. Though he played only twice on the winning side in a World Series, he was to make up for that as a manager.

Stengel could not have known it in the fall of 1916, but he was to play in Brooklyn for only one more season. His average fell to .257 in 1917 and, though

47

he was still a favorite of both the fans and the management, he was considered expendable. In an effort to get help for their pitching staff, the Dodgers traded him to Pittsburgh on January 9, 1918. It was but the close of a single chapter. Casey would appear again on the bizarre stage of Ebbets Field.

4.

CASEY MADE his return to Brooklyn a memorable one. It was one of the few occasions on which he resorted to the use of a partner in his act but, since ornithology has established that his partner was a sparrow, this has not been held against him. A large crowd was on hand that spring afternoon in 1918 when the Pirates made their first visit of the season to Brooklyn. Many in the crowd had come to see their old favorite, Stengel, and, being Brooklyn fans, their behavior was, of course, unpredictable. To Casey's astonishment he was received not with the cheers which a crowd might reasonably be expected to accord an old friend, but with a variety of jeers and catcalls. Casey's past heroics had been forgotten; what counted now was that he wore an enemy uniform, and no enemy could be welcomed in Brooklyn.

The jeers had been loud when he went to the outfield in the first inning. He made his first appearance at bat in the second inning and the hostile noises increased in intensity. As he was about to step into the batter's box, Stengel turned and doffed his cap to the crowd. It was a spectacular gesture. A sparrow darted out of the cap and flew away over the infield.

The most adamant Dodger fan must have cheered that performance. Afterward, Casey was asked by a still badly shaken press where he had found the sparrow. "Leon Cadore (a Dodger pitcher) picked it up in the grass. Somebody said it had hit the wall and stunned itself. Anyway, I asked Cadore to give it to me and I stuck it under my cap. It began to come back to life and it kicked up such a fuss under there I didn't think my cap would stay on my head till I could get up to the plate."

"I always knew he had birds in his attic," was Uncle Robbie's reaction.

Stengel found himself back in Brooklyn before he could establish himself in Pittsburgh. His orders came not from baseball's overlords, but from the Navy Department, which had a priority on Casey's services. World War I was already draining off the majors' top stars. Feeling that his bandy legs were not suited for marching under a full pack, Casey wisely joined the Navy in 1918 and, to his delight, was assigned to duty at the Brooklyn Navy Yard. Some young officer, manifestly touched by genius, believed he saw in Stengel the qualities of leadership that would make him a good baseball manager.

So Stengel fought his war in congenial surroundings, providing the Navy Yard with a respectable ball team and reaping the benefits of his exalted position by eating in the officers' mess. Shore leave for Casey meant renewing friendships in his old haunts along Fulton Street. It was then that an astounded world (or that portion of it closely connected with the Brooklyn Navy Yard) first glimpsed those qualities of managerial astuteness that Stengel was later to exhibit when he became the leader of the mighty

50

Yankees. "I arranged my own schedule," he said, "and so I made it my business to board every ship as it came in, and I scheduled a game with their team for the next day. That way we got them before they could get rid of their sea legs. I think we'd be winning yet if they didn't go and call off the war."

Only one sour note marred Casey's war with the Kaiser. His team played its game at the Parade Grounds in Brooklyn, and one day Stengel discovered on his arrival there that he had thirty-seven dollars in his pocket. Because both teams dressed in the same clubhouse, he was reluctant to leave the money in his navy blues. He gave it to the batboy, asking that young man to hold it for him until after the game. When the game started, Casey took his position in the outfield. Suddenly a disconcerting sight came to his roving eyes. He saw a bicycle proceeding away from the Parade Grounds in considerable haste, pedaled by a youth who looked suspiciously like the batboy. Casey had not only lost his thirty-seven dollars, but between innings he had to rustle up another boy to handle the bats. "The moral of that story," Casey concludes, "is never trust a boy on a bicycle."

The war over, Stengel returned to the Pirates, but his career there was not as pleasant as it had been in Brooklyn, nor was it to be as long. Casey believed, with some justification, that he was an established big-leaguer and should be paid as one. The Pirates' owner, Barney Dreyfuss, held what Casey considered reactionary views on the amount of money to be doled out to his hired help. Casey had some things to say to Dreyfuss on the matter, but that gentleman was

51

too busy counting his money to hear him. It was not long before Stengel did come to Dreyfuss' attention, however. Watching Casey in the outfield, he began to get the impression that he had lost interest in his work. Even the bleacher fans were abusing Stengel for what they felt was a pronounced absence of hustle, and Casey gave them no reason to change their opinion. After taking his time fielding a long hit one afternoon and subsequently hearing about it from the leather-lunged jury behind him, he turned and bellowed to the crowd: "What do you expect from a fella who's starving to death?"

Right or wrong (and it was the only time Casey has been accused of not giving his best to his profession), Dreyfuss soon felt that his outspoken right-fielder would be happier in other surroundings. Early in September, he switched outfielders in mid-stream, trading Casey to Philadelphia for George Whitten. However, while his salary apparently was adjusted to correspond more closely with his appraisal of himself, Casey found his position not much improved in other respects. The Phillies finished in last place in the three seasons he played for them.

That the Phillies were the doormats of the league was not Stengel's fault. He was one of the league's better outfielders, finishing the 1919 season with a .293 average and batting .292 for them in 1920.

It is well-known in baseball that a player's little aches and pains increase in intensity as his team plummets in the standings. Stengel's were no exception. As age crept up on him, his back began to ache, while at the same time the Phillies' leftfielder, Irish Meusel, was afflicted with a sore arm. Centerfielder Cy Williams was obliged to carry the burden and Stengel and Meusel urged him on from either side with cries of "Come on, Cy!" It became their battlecry.

Casey had other troubles in addition to the pain in his back. His locker was next to that of Bill Donovan, the manager of the hapless Phillies. The pitiful sighs and groans which the manager emitted after each losing game touched even Stengel's sensibilities. Because the pain in his back threatened to keep him out of the lineup for another two weeks in July of that year, 1921, Casey also had to endure the reproachful glances of Donovan. In self-defense, he decided to remove his belongings to another locker in the rear of the clubhouse. One rainy afternoon Casey was sitting in front of his new locker waiting for the game to be cancelled. Jimmy Hagan, then secretary of the Phillies, walked in and asked, "Where's Stengel?"

"He's dressing back there now," one of the players said.

"Oh, yeah?" Hagan said. "Well, he'll be dressing further off than that after today."

As Hagan was the customary bearer of the news when a player was to be shipped to the minors, there was a stir in the clubhouse.

"Oh-oh!" Casey said to himself. "Peoria."

The other players watched in silence as Hagan spoke softly with Stengel. Suddenly the invalid leaped into the air, clicked his heels together and threw himself into a dance of joy that would have been the wonder

53

of the most agile ballerina. "I've been traded to the Giants!" he shouted. "My back's all right! When's the next train to New York?"

There was good reason for Stengel's joy. The Giants had behind them a tradition of greatness, and their manager, John McGraw, was then assembling a team which was to surpass all of their past triumphs. No faith healer could have done as much for Stengel's infirmities as the news that he was on his way to New York. The next day a Giant pitcher was standing near the clubhouse door when Stengel passed through on his way to the field. Not aware that anyone was close to him, Casey slapped himself hard on the chest, arms and legs and said, "Wake up, muscles! We're in New York now!"

And so there came together two of the most colorful men the game was to know and, in the opinion of many fans and writers, its two greatest managers. McGraw, like Robbie, had played with the Baltimore Orioles in the Nineties, and had managed them for a season. He was brought to New York as pilot of the Giants in the summer of 1902 and his teams dominated the National League in the first quarter of this century.

He was an alert, daring leader, scathing and stern in his own clubhouse, combative and unrelenting on the field. That he could manage today's union-conscious players, who so carefully cultivate their individual rights, is doubtful, for his invective was unrelieved by the humor with which Stengel draws the sting from his own critical monologues. The "Little

Napoleon," as he was known, was the most respected and hated man in baseball.

By the time Stengel arrived at the Polo Grounds, McGraw had won six pennants there and finished second eight times. In 1921 the Giants were to win the first of four straight flags, a feat then without precedent. It was only natural that McGraw should exert a tremendous influence on Stengel. Henceforth Casey would always be a "McGraw man" and he used his old master's methods even when others believed the modern game had made them obsolete. It cannot be said that the influence was mutual. While McGraw knew Stengel as a good clutch player and a smart veteran, he realized that he was now in his thirties and had passed his peak; he was to be only a part-time player with the Giants. It is suspected that McGraw also looked on him as a clown and a "Goodtime Charley" who could occasionally help the club on the field. Neither McGraw nor anyone else around the Giants saw in Casey the raw material of a manager who would in time fashion a record greater even than his master's.

The Giants of that era were a lusty crew whose spirit and habits matched those of Stengel. There were great players such as Frankie Frisch and Ross Youngs and Dave Bancroft; there were players who made pleasant companions for Casey as he roamed New York, Chicago, Cincinnati and the other National League cities after dark; and there were rough-and-ready battlers on whom one could count when fists began to fly, on or off the playing field. As one of their number had said, "It's great to be young and a Giant."

There is in existence a memorable photograph of Casey being led off the field, capless and still raging, by two policemen after trying to flatten a pitcher named Phil Weinert. A pitch had come suspiciously close to Stengel's head. He had taken brush-back pitches in stride when he was a rookie, but he obviously felt that age and seniority now entitled him to some measure of respect. He delivered a manifesto to that effect to Weinert, and when the pitcher told Casey to go soak his head he rushed to the mound and attempted to knock some of the disrespect out of him. Nobody ever questioned Casey's ardor for battle, but his skill as a pugilist left something to be desired. The law finally pulled the two combatants apart before anything more than feelings had been damaged.

Another time, not recorded on film, Casey did not fare so well. Adolph Luque, a rough and fearless Cuban, was pitching against New York. Seated next to Stengel in the dugout was another Giant outfielder, Bill Cunningham. The Giants took delight in taunting the big Cuban, and on this day the bench jockeying grew particularly vicious. Suddenly Luque jammed his glove into his pocket and rushed over to the Giant bench. Casey, believing Cunningham was the target of the enraged Cuban, sat back to watch the slaughter. Luque walked right past Cunningham, and punched the amazed Stengel in the eye. Luque may have picked the wrong man, but even Casey had to admit that he was the most likely suspect.

Dispensing and receiving lusty wallops was a natural

part of any Giant player's routine. Casey has said of the Giants of that era, "When they couldn't find anybody else to fight, they kept in practice punching each other around."

He came close to becoming a victim of fratricidal warfare himself. He once told Jack Scott, one of the Giant pitchers, that he couldn't play center field behind Scott.

"Why not?" asked Scott.

"Your ears are too big," said Stengel, breaking into a grin. "I can't see the ball leave the bat."

Like Falstaff, Casey had heard the chimes at midnight. No one knew it better than McGraw. Irish Meusel had also come to the Giants from Philadelphia and he and Casey played havoc with McGraw's curfew. For a time the manager could keep tabs on this carefree pair because he had assigned a detective to follow them. Then one day the detective reported to McGraw that the warm friendship between the two had apparently come to an end. They no longer went out with each other. Puzzled, McGraw mentioned it to Casey at the Polo Grounds. "Why did you stop going out with Meusel?"

"I'm particular," Casey said. "I don't want to share a detective with anybody."

During a losing streak, more annoying to McGraw than harmful to the Giants' pennant chances, the fiery manager decided that the after-hours carousing had gone far enough. He had caught three or four of the culprits in the act and was berating them savagely in the clubhouse one day before a game. Stengel, whose behavior happened to be exemplary at that time (or

57

so he later claimed), had come straight from the barber shop to the ball park. Unfortunately, the barber had applied a heavy dose of bay rum to his rugged features. As he entered the clubhouse, McGraw sniffed, wheeled about and transfixed the astonished Casey. "At it too, eh, Stengel?" he roared. "All right. You're fined fifty dollars."

McGraw was driving his players fiercely now. While the Giants had dominated baseball in New York as far back as anyone could remember, both in skill and in glamour, that ascendancy was now being threatened by the Yankees. Babe Ruth had arrived in New York, and around him the Yankees were building a team that in time would become the greatest the game has known. For a while McGraw was able to hold them off. The Giants won pennants in 1921 and 1922, defeating the Yankees both years in the World Series. Stengel, though he didn't play every day, became an even more consistent hitter than he had been in Brooklyn. His batting average, which had been .284 in 1921 when he divided the season between Philadelphia and New York, soared to .368 in the eighty-four games he played in 1922. He came to bat only five times in the World Series that year (he had not played in the 1921 Series) and got two hits for a .400 average.

Casey spent the winter of 1922-23 in California. When the day arrived on which he was to leave for the Giants' training camp at San Antonio, Texas, he got in touch with teammates who were also in California and agreed to meet them at the railroad station in order that they might travel as a group. The wives of several of the players were at the station to see their husbands off and with them was an attractive young lady named Edna Lawson. Casey was mightily impressed. All through the summer months that followed he carried on a transcontinental courtship, using the long distance telephone and special delivery mail. His carefree days as a bachelor were rapidly running out.

Casey had a distinct advantage over the other suitors for Edna's hand. Her father, a wealthy Glendale, California, real estate man, had seen a picture of Casey in the paper and was immediately won over. "Dad noticed," Edna said, "that Casey had bow legs, just like his favorite player, Hans Wagner." Who could ask for a more favorable introduction to a future father-in-law?

There was still another pennant to be won and the Giants, heavy favorites, were not going to let it get away from them. They beat back determined surges by the Reds and Pirates and were in command of the league as the season came to an end. Casey was once more a handy utility player. He batted .339 in 75 games, and McGraw, counting on his skill and resourcefulness, put him in the regular lineup as the Giants again met the Yankees in the World Series.

It is ironic that Stengel was the Giant player who put up the most heroic individual battle as the Yankees moved in to take the Series and begin their long domination of baseball. Stengel fired two mighty shots and then the Giants fell back, relinquishing their claim to be the number one ball club in the greatest city in the world. The Yankee victory in 1923 was the first of seventeen world championship flags which were to fly over the mammoth stadium they had opened that spring. The Giants, while they enjoyed occasional success in the years to come, never recaptured the glory of those days under McGraw, and their fortunes waned until they eventually disappeared completely from the city they had once ruled.

Stengel kept his finger in the dike for a few wonderful days in 1923. The baseball season, with its arduous exhibition trek in the spring and its 154-game schedule, can seem interminable to a player after he has struggled through ten or more such years. As the Series began Casey's muscles ached and he wore a sponge rubber cushion in one shoe to ease the pain of a bad bone bruise. But his minor ailments were forgotten in the excitement of the moment. The opener on October 10 was the first World Series game ever played at Yankee Stadium and a crowd of over 55,000 festive spectators gave added incentive to the 33-year-old Casey. For eight innings the two bitterly rival teams battled on even terms and when the Giants came to bat in the top of the ninth the score was tied, 4-4. With Bullet Joe Bush pitching for the Yankees, Casey lined one of his fast balls far over the head of Bob Meusel in left-center field. The crowd came to its feet with a tremendous roar as the ball hit the ground and rolled toward the distant bleacher wall. A few years before it would have been an easy inside-the-park home run for Casey; now the most optimistic Giant fan gave Stengel's weary legs little chance to score against the strong arm of Meusel.

Casey rounded second base at high speed and was nearly overtaken by disaster. "I thought my shoe fell off," he said later. It was only the rubber cushion which had popped out of the shoe. Winded and limping, he rounded third base and, after what seemed an eternity to him and to the roaring Giant fans, he staggered across the plate, seconds ahead of the throw, with the winning run. The Giants held off the Yankees in the bottom of the ninth and won the important opening game, 5-4.

A large corps of sports writers present for the historic game immediately set to work immortalizing Stengel's feat in the most lyrical prose at its command. This was a happy sequel to "Casey At The Bat." Carried away by the drama of Stengel's vital smash, the writers vividly pictured this baseball relic who had come off the bench to add his name to the list of World Series titans. They described the magnitude of his blow and the desperate dash of this veteran, bowed by the weight of years, as he galumphed around the bases to defeat both time and Meusel's arm. Some, with poetic license, imagined Casey trailing a long white beard behind him as he rounded third and set sail for the plate. It may have been lurid journalism, but that was the "Golden Age" of sport and the enthusiasm of fan and writer alike was boundless.

The fanciful reports of this baseball Methuselah were duly noted 3,000 miles away. Edna Lawson, having excitedly read of her fiancé's heroics, took the newspapers to her father. He read them with interest and then put them down.

"Well, Pops," Edna asked, "what do you think of my Casey now?"

He flashed a look of pity at his daughter and shook his head. "I hope," he said, "that your Casey lives until the wedding."

The Giants lost the second game at the Polo Grounds and the two clubs went back across the Harlem River to Yankee Stadium with one victory apiece. For six innings the third game remained a scoreless tie as Arthur Nehf dueled Sam Jones of the Yankees. Then, in the seventh inning, the god of aged ballplayers smiled once more on Stengel. Casey hammered a pitch into the rightfield bleachers for his second home run of the Series. As he rounded the bases he looked into the Yankee dugout, then behind third base, and delivered to them a gesture of contempt—he thumbed his nose.

Nehf, pitching brilliantly, went on to shut out the Yankees that afternoon, 1-0. The Giant partisans were deliriously happy and Stengel was the toast of that portion of New York which still refused to concede that Babe Ruth and his teammates were anything more than bumptious upstarts. Col. Jacob Ruppert, the owner of the Yankees, did not concur in the general homage paid to Stengel. His sensibilities had been outraged by the vulgar gesture Casey had directed at his ball club. He lodged an immediate protest with Judge Kenesaw M. Landis, the Commissioner of Baseball, and demanded suitable punishment for what he felt was an insult to the fans as well as to his players. Landis, a fire-breathing tyrant in most of his official decisions, ignored Ruppert's protest. If it wasn't the defiant gesture of a gallant warrior in the face of fearful odds, it was at most a harmless faux pas. After all, what else could one expect from a clown like Stengel?

No one has ever relished victory more than Casey, and he did not let pass the opportunity to make the most of it. Surrounded by reporters in the clubhouse, he bellowed, "That makes two games for Stengel and one game for the Yankees." Then, with an assumed expression of puzzlement, he asked, "Say, whatever became of the Giants?"

He was not to know such glory again for more than a quarter of a century. His star, like that of the Giants, was waning as the Yankees' rose, and to taste success once more he would have to accede to that celebrated dictum of an anonymous wise man: "If you can't lick 'em, join 'em!" At the end of the third game, the Giants had spent their ammunition. They would not win another in the 1923 Series. Led by the great Babe Ruth, the Yankees stormed back to win three straight games and clinch the Series, 4-2. They couldn't take those two victories from Stengel, but now the writers were repeating his question—what, indeed, had become of the Giants?

Soon after the World Series, McGraw left with his wife on a trip to Europe. Before sailing, he completed a deal that ended Casey's days with the Giants. The Boston Braves wanted the Giants' shortstop, Bancroft, to manage their team. Not wishing to stand in his way, McGraw sent Bancroft, Stengel and Cunningham to Boston in exchange for Billy Southworth and Joe Oeschger. Did the Giants' manager feel Stengel had reached an age at which he could be of no further help to the team? Or did he merely want to rid the club of one of the ringleaders of the Giants' after-dark brigade?

Stengel believed the latter reason prompted McGraw to include him in the package deal with the Braves, and at first he was bitter about it. He felt that the blame had in many cases fallen on him unjustly. "What does a fella have to do to make good in this league?" he complained to a friend. "I suppose if I hadda hit three home runs in the Series they'd have packed me off to the Three-Eye League."

Later, he could be more philosophical about his abrupt departure from the Polo Grounds. "The paths of glory lead but to the Braves," he intoned. Or so it is alleged.

5.

MIDDLE AGE, which begins to take hold of him in his early thirties, is a bleak period for the big league ballplayer. He is probably then at the peak of his career and his income has increased with his achievements and years of service. He is a national celebrity, he and his family have a reasonably high standard of living, and he experiences the pleasures anyone derives from having mastered a difficult profession. Then, suddenly his entire way of life is sharply altered. The fine reflexes, those indispensable tools of the athlete, grow dull. His high salary makes him a liability to his employers who have a flock of eager, strong-armed young men, all earning one-fifth or even one-tenth of what his contract calls for, and all ready to move in and take his job. Once in a great while a player steps into one of the sixteen big league managing posts at the end of his playing career; but that is extremely rare, and those who have no other trade but baseball usually return as managers or players to the bush leagues from which they had climbed so painfully.

This was the prospect facing Stengel as he left the Giants. Today's player, who is more akin to a young industrial executive than to the crude bruisers of an earlier era, often has a lucrative business opportunity awaiting him if he elects not to remain in baseball. Casey at that time had no other choice. He had renounced the sprinkling cart; vaudeville had been only a fleeting dream; and there was no place in our society for a lefthanded dentist. He could not, in any case, have voluntarily given up baseball. It was then, as it is today, the biggest thing in his life. But it hurt him to realize that he, a World Series hero against the Yankees, would soon be too old for the big leagues. Boston was almost certainly the last stop in his playing career.

1924 was Casey's Indian Summer as a player. With Boston he was a regular again, something he hadn't been since 1920 in Philadelphia, and he batted .280 in 131 games. It was like being with Philadelphia in other respects, too—the Braves finished a feeble last. It must have been a blow to Casey's ego to see that he could play regularly only on eighth-place teams. There was a measure of solace for him in all this, though; Edna came East, and they were married in August.

Later in the 1924 season he got another chance to perform a service for his old boss, McGraw, when for a moment he was a great clutch player again. The Giants' drive for a fourth straight National League pennant was seriously challenged only by their ancient arch-rivals, the Dodgers, who were still hot on their heels as the season entered its waning days. The Dodgers' hopes were finally stilled when the last-place Braves rose up and knocked them out of contention, the big blow being dealt by Stengel, whose tenth inning single with the bases filled drove in the winning runs.

In the fall of 1924 there was a brief reunion with McGraw, who managed a National League all-star team which made a round-the-world exhibition tour with a similar squad from the American League. England was the high point of the tour for Casey, a member of the National League team, and for Edna. A game was played at Stamford Bridge, Yorkshire, where King George V and his son, the future George VI, were among the spectators. Stengel, who had not been intimidated by the denizens of the Ginney Flats in Brooklyn, was surely not likely to be awed by royalty. Taking advantage of the occasion, he hit a home run to help defeat the American Leaguers. To Casey's dismay, George Bernard Shaw, covering the game for a London paper, was not impressed by his long hit. Shaw, like most of the English and Irish spectators, found the fielding a more intriguing aspect of the game than the hitting. Casey has had his revenge; he prefers *The Sporting News* to *Saint Joan*.

The itinerant all-stars continued their tour around the globe, but Stengel did not distinguish himself again until they reached Manila. At an official reception there, he was called upon to say a few words. The microphone had not then become a common crutch of feeble-throated orators. This was one of the few recorded episodes in which Casey was reluctant to test either the volume or the durability of his vocal cords. Facing the large assembly of guests, he launched into an impassioned diatribe that contained gestures, grimaces, posturings and fiery glances—indeed all of the standard implements of the rhetorician but words. Unheard melodies are sweetest, the poet claims, and Casey proved that day that unheard words can stir the multitude. When at last he spoke his phantom peroration and sat down, he was accorded a tumultuous ovation.

Casey's big league playing career came to an abrupt end in the spring of 1925. He had begun the season as a pinch-hitter for Boston, but soon was called aside by Judge Emil Fuchs, who owned the Braves.

"Casey," Fuchs said, "we've bought the Worcester club as a farm team. We'd like you to run the operation there for us. You'll be the manager, and you'll also have the title of president of the club. Will you take it?"

It was an easy decision for Stengel to make. Naturally, he did not like to leave the big leagues, but he was quick to detect the handwriting on the wall. Apparently even the desperate Braves believed he had outlived his usefulness as a player. Here was an opportunity to manage his own ball club. "I'll take it, Judge," Casey said. Thus he entered the second and most glittering stage of his career. He was a manager.

The Worcester, Massachusetts, team was then in the Eastern League and when Casey arrived there on May 22, he was made to feel right at home; Worcester was in last place. The Braves contributed a couple of pretty good players to the roster, Casey added liveliness and his stout bat to the lineup, and Worcester began to rise in the standings. At that time Stengel made a friendship that was to play an important role in his later life. George Weiss, the man who hired him to manage the Yankees in the fall of 1948, was the general manager of the New Haven team in the

Eastern League. Though they were rival executives, they often whiled away evenings talking baseball. The general admiration in which Weiss is held today surely rests partly on the durability he displayed on those evenings long ago with Stengel.

"I guess," Weiss has said in a nostalgic moment, "I have stayed up later and talked longer—or, rather, listened longer—with Casey than with anybody else in baseball. You know how he is and how he can use up the hours of a night and still be going strong when it's daylight. If you weren't a baseball man, why, you'd think the guy was crazy. But if you were, when you finally got to bed—and the chances are he'd still be sitting on the other bed and still talking—it wouldn't take you long to find out you were really learning things." Weiss has never forgotten those nights.

When the Eastern League season came to a close Stengel could look back on his record there with modest satisfaction. His team had finished in third place and he had batted .320 in 100 games. Weiss was not the only baseball man who had been impressed by Casey's progress as a manager. During the winter, Stengel received an attractive offer to manage Toledo in the American Association. It was a step upward. He applied to Fuchs for a release from his managerial contract at Worcester on the grounds that he had a chance to better himself, but Fuchs refused to grant it to him. The Judge knew that in Stengel he possessed the services of a remarkable baseball man. He did not realize, however, the extent of Casey's resourcefulness. Charles Dillon Stengel, the president of the Worcester team, promptly dispatched a letter to Casey Stengel, manager of the Worcester team, informing him that he had been dismissed from his position. Then president Stengel, who had no contract, notified Fuchs that he had resigned.

Judge Fuchs was outraged. So was Baseball Commissioner Landis. He told Fuchs that he would declare Stengel's act "null and void," but Fuchs' declined Landis' assistance. "If that's the way Stengel wants it," the Boston owner wrote to Landis, "let him go. We're better off without him."

For a time there was a rumor in baseball that Stengel's evasion of his contract had so angered Landis that Casey would never again be permitted to work in the big leagues. Those rumors proved to be false, but there is no doubt of the bitterness with which both Landis and Fuchs regarded Stengel.

The years in Toledo were pleasant ones for Casey. He and Edna made many friends there, and they have talked about the city often in the years which followed. Most of Casey's memories, of course, have a baseball background. It was a good league and he occasionally had fine players to work with. Although his teams ran the gamut of performance from the best to the worst, he kept adding to his stature as a manager. He still loves to recall the days when Toledo beat the superb minor league teams which Joe McCarthy had put together at Louisville. Their recollection was later a source of consolation for him when, while he managed miserable teams at Brooklyn and Boston in the Thirties, McCarthy dominated the baseball world as the manager of the awesome Yankees.

Casey had an opportunity to display all phases of his genius at Toledo. The farm system did not play as great a role in baseball then as it does today, and the majority of minor league teams were independently owned. A principal source of their income was from the sale of players to the big leagues. Casey was adept at fattening his players for the market. If he had a pitcher he felt he could sell at the end of the season he used him wisely, showing him off regularly against the weaker clubs and hiding him when the more formidable teams came to town. He occasionally held salable young sluggers out of the lineup when Toledo was faced by pitchers who might shave valuable points off their batting averages. The Toledo treasury flourished during Stengel's tenure there.

Stengel also knew how to save money for the club. Once when a young player had joined the team after graduating from college, Casey was cornered in the clubhouse by one of the veterans.

"Look, I was four years getting to this club," the player said, "bouncing around in the bushes, eating lousy food, riding buses all night and getting nickels and dimes. Now I find out this kid playing alongside me comes right in here from college and gets more dough than me. I want a raise."

Casey rubbed his chin and made a face. "Let's look at it this way," he said to the unhappy player. "This fella went to college for four years to learn to play second base. He had to pay his own expenses, and his tuition there and his room and board. In four years he must have spent about five grand. Where were you those four years? Getting paid for learning.

You never spent a cent for it. Now, what's your squawk?"

Tradition has it that the veteran hung his head, mumbled, "I never thought of that," and walked away.

Stengel won a pennant in Toledo in 1927, but in other seasons his teams finished anywhere from third to last. It was an era of prosperity and at times it seemed to him that his players were more interested in their gains in the stock market than their batting averages. One day he walked into the clubhouse and discovered a group looking over the financial page of a newspaper and discussing the day's developments in Wall Street.

"Fellas," he said, with the air of a man who knows, "I've got a good tip for you. Buy all the Pennsylvania Railroad stock you can get your hands on."

"No fooling, Casey?" one of the players asked. "How do you know?"

"I know," Stengel roared, "that when we start shipping you guys back to the bushes next week the railroads is going to get rich!"

Casey scored one triumph at Toledo that has gone unrecorded. "I only won one fight in my life," he says proudly, "and that was at Toledo. There was a man in the bleachers was on me very bad one day and after the game was over I hunted him down and pulled him under the stands and flattened him. But I really lost that one, too. They fined me a hundred dollars and suspended me for ten days."

When his team finished in last place in 1931, Stengel must have thought that this was where he had come in. The country was in the grip of the depression by then, and there seemed little chance of any improvement in the Toledo club's fortunes. At about this same time, Max Carey, who had played in the outfield with Casey at Pittsburgh, was appointed manager of the Dodgers, replacing Wilbert Robinson. Stengel saw the opportunity to disengage himself from his unhappy plight at Toledo and step back into a big league uniform. He applied for a job as a coach with the Dodgers. There was a brief delay while the Brooklyn front office investigated the old rumor that Landis would not permit Stengel's return to the majors and, finding it without foundation, informed Casey that he was hired. This marked the end of Stengel's playing career, for he had sometimes pinch-hit at Toledo.

While the Dodgers had done well financially, they had suffered artistically. Ebbets Field had become a refuge for aged, infirm, and incompetent players. Above all, it had attracted the most bizarre assemblage of clowns ever to bedevil a manager and confuse the opposition. To a report that the Dodgers had three men on base, the standard reply was, "Which base?"

Uncle Robbie, either oblivious of what was going on around him or numbed by the endless parody on baseball presented by his teams, had borne up remarkably well. "The Daffiness Boys" they were called, but Robbie could point with pride to the high attendance figures, which indicated that, while they were poor players indeed, they were Brooklyn's own. Although their incompetence was sometimes frightening, it was often relieved by some powerful batting displays, for, whatever the flaws of the Daffiness Boys in the field or on the bases, they could make life miserable for enemy pitchers. In the front office the incompetence was unrelieved. The club's officers passed their days in wrangling among themselves, or with Uncle Robbie, and seldom found time to provide new ballplayers for the foundering team. Uncle Robbie had finally been forced out, and Carey, a sober and industrious baseball man, was hired to replace him.

A coach may fill several functions with a ball club. He can be a teacher, well grounded in the fundamentals of baseball, which he transmits to the younger players. Or he can be a factotum, keeping track of balls, passing down orders from the top, and serving as a confidant to the manager. Stengel was qualified to play either role, but his performance was necessarily limited. Most of the players were too old to learn new tricks or simply impervious to education of any sort. Stengel, however, was a loyal coach, and if he did not materially aid the Dodgers, who were beyond help, he certainly did not hinder the players or do anything to undermine Carey's command. He was happy to be back in the big leagues and content to let Carey run the show.

It was well for Casey that he didn't become too prominent a part of the Carey regime. Evil days had overtaken the Dodgers. They were still losing ball games, but under the leadership of Carey they were losing in an orthodox fashion, seemingly having forgotten how to bring about their own downfall through absurd or muddle-headed misplays. This was

74

an affront to their loyal fans. The citizens of Brooklyn would come to Ebbets Field with faint hopes that their heroes would win, and in the course of the afternoon they would jeer their mistakes. They would not come to Ebbets Field to see the Dodgers lose just like any other team.

In 1933, when the Dodgers plummeted to sixth place and attendance at the park took a sharp dip, there were rumors that Carey would be fired. The Dodgers' front office promptly denied them and reinforced its denial by re-signing him to manage the Dodgers in 1934. After the season Casey returned to Glendale, where he and Edna made their home, and impatiently awaited the coming of spring. Late in February he was notified to report to Brooklyn for an important conference. Believing that Carey, who had spent the winter in Miami Beach, would also be present, and that the conference had been called to discuss some of the new players on the roster, Stengel left for Brooklyn.

He did not know that the Brooklyn directors had privately chosen him as the new manager of the Dodgers. To cover up their own failure to supply Carey with major league ballplayers, the directors had agreed among themselves to give Max his release, thereby shifting the blame, by inference, to his already sagging shoulders, and to hire Stengel, who had always been popular with the writers, to silence any criticism of their methods. On arriving at the Dodgers' office on Montague Street, Casey was surprised to find that Carey was missing.

"Where's Max?" he asked.

There was a general shuffling of feet and clearing of throats. Then one of the club's directors spoke up. "Casey, we want you to manage the Dodgers."

Stengel blinked and looked around him. "But where's Carey?"

"That's just it. We've decided to let Max go. Do you want the job?"

"But Max is my friend. He gave me my job here. What about his contract for this year?"

"He will be paid off. Don't worry about Carey. He's gone. Do you want the job?"

Stengel was silent for a moment. "But does he know about this?"

The directors assured him that Carey had been notified of his dismissal.

"Get him on the phone," Stengel said. "I want to talk to him."

A call was placed to Carey in Florida. He had been notified only minutes before Stengel arrived at Montague Street, and he was bitter at the shabby way he had been disposed of. "But never mind that, Casey," he said. "That's over now. You take the job, or they'll only give it to somebody else. I'm disgusted with them, not you."

When he had hung up, Casey turned to the directors. "All right," he said, "I'll take the job."

So Stengel signed to manage the Dodgers for $15,000 a year, less than Carey was being paid *not* to manage them. He must have known he would hold his post by no very certain tenure. He knew the men who hired him, he had seen how they had treated Carey, and he knew the players they would place at his dis-

76

posal. Still, there would be laughs and excitement and that was part of Casey's life, too. He had embarked on perhaps the strangest adventure of an extraordinary career.

6.

"Is BROOKLYN still in the league?"

At the sound of those words Brooklyn, strangely somnolent throughout the two seasons of Max Carey's reign, erupted violently in the winter of 1934. It all began innocently enough. Bill Terry, who had succeeded John McGraw as the manager of the Giants, guided his team to the pennant and world championship in 1933. During the baseball meetings at the Roosevelt Hotel in New York the following February, Terry was answering the routine questions of a group of writers. Roscoe McGowen of the New York *Times* asked him his opinion of the Dodgers' prospects for the coming year.

Terry smiled complacently at McGowen and asked, "Is Brooklyn still in the league?"

Terry may have thought it mildly funny, but Brooklyn fans didn't. Their zeal then was tempered by neither a surfeit of success nor the spectre of Los Angeles. Proud and combative, they would permit no outsider to insult their "Bums." When, soon afterward, Stengel replaced the deposed Carey, he inherited the obligation to wipe the smirk from Terry's face. There was excitement in Brooklyn once again. Terry had violated one half the capsule philosophy of a sagacious football coach: "Avoid the tough opponents and don't get the easy ones mad at you."

78

It was an unimpressive crew that presented itself for Casey's inspection at the team's spring training camp in Orlando. Sprinkled among the nonentities were a few players of talent; Al Lopez, a catcher, Tony Cuccinello, an infielder, and Van Lingle Mungo, a large, eccentric pitcher who matched Bugs Baer's description of another hard-throwing young man: "He could throw a lamb chop past a wolf."

Casey knew that at best they couldn't go very far. Looking them over, he could pick out a bloodshot eye here and an unnaturally red nose there and his experience warned him he had better ride herd on some of them or risk the team's complete collapse. "I'm not going to stand up and say you men can't have a glass of grog for a toothache once in a while," he told them. "But don't let me catch one of you going out of the hotel after midnight to mail a letter. This club is paying for your hotel rooms, and we want you to use them once in a while."

Rules were made to be broken, as Eve was undoubtedly the first to point out, and Casey soon detected one of his athletes returning to the hotel long after midnight. The player had a reasonably plausible story and Casey heard it through to the end. Then he sighed and shook his head. "That's a good story," he said. "Yes, that's a very good story. In fact, I told it to McGraw just about this same hour of the morning back in 1922. Now, McGraw fined me fifty dollars that night, but seeing as how times ain't so good, I'm only going to charge you twenty-five."

Casey led his tattered legions north and opened a memorable season. He knew they would flounder in the end, but it would be a feather in his cap if he could pull the Giants down with him. In Brooklyn Bill Terry had become the symbol of all that was distasteful, and whenever he appeared in Ebbets Field the fans booed him unmercifully. They were not going to let Terry forget those words tossed off so lightly in February.

Stengel struggled along with the castoffs and mediocrities he had inherited from Carey. One such castoff was Hack Wilson, a fearsome slugger in his day, but his day had long since passed. With the disappearance of his skills, Hack had lost some of his interest in the game. The Dodgers were playing the Phillies in tiny Baker Bowl one afternoon when Casey's starting pitcher, the aptly named "Boom Boom" Beck, began to take a terrible pounding. Stengel trudged to the mound to inform his pitcher that he might have the remainder of the day off. Beck disagreed with Stengel's estimate of his effectiveness. "I still got my stuff, Casey," he protested.

"Maybe you've got your stuff," Stengel said wearily, "but they're hitting it. Give me the ball."

While Casey and Boom Boom discussed the quality of the latter's fast ball, Wilson, stationed in right field, had lapsed into upright unconsciousness. Finally realizing he had lost the argument, Beck turned in disgust and threw the ball down the first base line where it bounced against the close right field wall. Wilson, hearing the bang of the ball against the face, concluded that someone had lined a base hit there while he was woolgathering. He raced after the ball, picked it up and made a perfect throw to second base. The crowd sent up a sarcastic cheer as Wilson pawed the ground in embarrassment. Stengel's only comment on the incident was: "I didn't know Boom Boom could throw the ball that far."

They were artless Dodgers indeed. Otto Miller, who had been a teammate of Casey's on the Dodger championship team of 1916, was the proprietor of a tavern in Brooklyn by the time Stengel returned as their manager, and he suffered through many long afternoons in the stands at Ebbets Field. Talking of those days, Miller said recently, "Casey reminded me of a guy who'd made up his mind to force a pair of deuces to beat four aces. And he never stopped trying."

Brooklyn's big moment arrived on the final weekend of the season. The Giants, just a step behind the league-leading Cardinals, had to beat the Dodgers in both of the games that made up the closing series at the Polo Grounds. To lose even once to the sixth place ragamuffins under Stengel's command would be a serious blow to their pennant chances. Fifty thousand fans, many of whom had followed their heroes over the bridge from Flatbush, packed the old Harlem ball park for Saturday's game. The Brooklyn fans howled insults at Terry and reminded him of his smug reply to the question posed by the gentleman from the *Times*. In the Brooklyn clubhouse Stengel gave his team its final instructions. And then: "Let's go! Let's show 'em we're still in the league—but not too still."

To Terry's unutterable discomfort, and the very articulate delight of thousands of Brooklyn residents,

Mungo throttled the Giants, 5-1. The Dodgers returned the following day to drive a stake through the heart of the still wriggling New Yorkers, 8-5. Terry, caught with his foot in his mouth, must have been tempted to put a pistol to his head. The Dodgers had finished sixth, but what did that matter when they had corked up the Giants in second place? Stengel, riding the subway back to Brooklyn after the final game, was held a prisoner in the car for over an hour by delirious Dodger fans who danced wildly around him and wouldn't let him escape until they had wrung every ounce of satisfaction from their glorious revenge.

It was the only triumph Stengel would know in Brooklyn. The rest was perpetual frustration against a background of farce. He spent three seasons at Ebbets Field and was never able to drive his cast of buffoons out of the second division, finishing sixth, fifth and seventh respectively. The Damoclean sword, wobbling above his head in the jittery fingers of the Dodgers' directors, must have seemed at times the one real thing in his life; at other times he must have looked to it as the only relief from the hopeless muddle in which he found himself. After one particularly messy game, he walked into a barber shop, settled back in the chair and said to the proprietor, "A haircut and a shave. But don't cut my throat. I might want to do that myself later."

Among the players who made up this cast of characters was Frenchy Bordagaray. Frenchy's distinguishing marks were a mustache and a goatee. When he appeared at spring training, peering out from behind his whiskers, Stengel took it as everybody else did —lightly. When a certain amount of time had passed and Frenchy still hadn't put himself into the hands of a barber, Casey hinted mildly that he didn't believe a big league diamond was the place for a goatee. "Anyway, Frenchy," he said, "it will only slow you down on the bases."

Bordagaray continued to cling proudly to his newest possession and Stengel resorted to intimidation. "I'm going to tell every catcher in the league to throw at your mustache when you're on the bases," he said darkly. Frenchy hurriedly complied with his manager's wishes and the mustache and goatee disappeared. It is hard to believe that Stengel ever lifted his hand to rob baseball of any of its color, but these are the facts.

Frenchy had been bought from the Pacific Coast League, and the Dodgers, who were hampered by, among other things, a glaring deficiency of speed, counted on his ability to run. As Tommy Holmes once wrote in the Brooklyn *Eagle*, "Frenchy's speed would have helped them had he run in the right direction."

In one game Frenchy arrived safely at second base. As the next batter took his place at the plate, the Chicago pitcher whirled and threw to the second baseman, Billy Herman. Frenchy was apparently standing on the base but, when Herman tagged him, the umpire shouted, "You're out!"

Stengel rushed from the Brooklyn dugout and raged at the umpire, protesting that Bordagaray couldn't possibly be out since his foot had been on the bag. The umpire refused to listen. Then Stengel became aware that Frenchy had walked back to the dugout, without saying a word in his own behalf. The frustrated Stengel raced after him and demanded, "Why weren't you out there arguing with me?"

"Well, Casey," Frenchy said, hanging his head, "I guess I was out."

"Out?" screamed Stengel. "How could you be out? You was standing on the bag!"

"Yeah, I was, but it was this way. While I was waiting for the pitcher to throw the ball I got a little bored and was tapping my foot. He must have got me between taps."

Another member of the Dodger team was Ox Eckhardt, a burly outfielder who had acquired a reputation as a devastating slugger in the minor leagues. The Dodgers bought him one winter and eagerly awaited his arrival at their spring training headquarters. At last a wire was received from Ox requesting the Dodgers to reserve a double room for him. Although rookies were not usually allowed to bring their wives to camp in those days, the Dodgers decided that they would make an exception in the case of this slugger who brought with him such an array of batting records. Ox showed up on schedule and Stengel and several Dodger officials were in the lobby of the hotel to greet him. They were about as surprised as anyone can be who has spent some time with the Dodgers when they saw Eckhardt walk in, trailing, not a wife, but an enormous St. Bernard on a leash.

"He always came to camp with me in the minors,"

Ox explained matter-of-factly, "and I thought he'd enjoy seeing a big league layout."

Another player the Dodgers' directors presented to Casey was Nick Tremark. Nick's distinguishing feature was the fact that he was only five feet, three inches tall. While he was of little help to the Dodgers, he did serve, like the sparrow, as a straight man for Casey's comedy routines. Whenever Nick got on base, Casey, standing in the coaching box behind third, would cup his hands around his eyes as if he were holding binoculars and peer about him for his tiny baserunner. It invariably drew a laugh from the crowd.

Stengel marveled at the efficient scouting systems which provided a constant stream of talent for the Cardinals and Yankees. During the winter meetings in St. Louis one year he was invited to look over the Cardinals' front office. In one room was a large map, in which colored pins had been stuck at the appropriate points to mark the locations of Cardinal farm teams. "I'm going to get some of them pins," Casey said. "I think we'll get good results by sticking them into our guys on the bench."

Casey never gave up in his efforts to give Brooklyn a winning team. He always looked to a future that he knew he would not be around Ebbets Field to enjoy. "But what do you do when you've got a second division ball club?" he once asked a reporter and then, naturally, went on to answer the question himself. "You've got a couple of young players on it. You work on them. What else are you gonna work on? You keep after them. You ask them why they didn't make that throw. You ask them why they played that man there. Then for somebody else they turn out to be good ballplayers, but what of it? You helped to make them good ballplayers, didn't you?"

The development of young players has always been as much of a passion with him as winning a pennant. While managing the Dodgers he supervised tryout camps for prospects in the mornings at Ebbets Field. He gave impromptu lectures to the assembled novices, watched them perform, and occasionally saw enough in one of them to sign him to a contract. It was during that period that he was first called "The Old Perfesser," apparently by Jerry Mitchell of the New York *Post*.

At one of those morning tryouts a little fellow named Phil Rizzuto showed up but he did not make an impression on anyone. "Too small," was the consensus, and Phil was sent on his way, which was to lead him to a brilliant career with the Yankees. Stengel now denies he was at that particular tryout, claiming that he was feuding with the Brooklyn directors at the time and had washed his hands of any extracurricular activities. Those who know Stengel will tell you that it is unlikely he ever shunned an opportunity to work with young players, regardless of the intensity of a feud or a hangover.

As manager of the Dodgers, time began to run out on Stengel in 1936. The Dodgers were struggling to stay a jump ahead of the bill collectors, and the shuffling and bickering in the front office was apparently leading the club to ruin. Joe DiMaggio came to the Yankee Stadium that year and the Yankees were surging toward the first of seven pennants they would capture in the next eight years. Bill Terry was leading the Giants to the first of two successive National League flags. Scrambling to keep out of last place, the Dodgers would rarely have been mentioned in the newspapers except for Stengel's capacities as a representative of good will to the outside world and the ingenuity displayed by his players in losing ball games. Also, the front office was not pleased by Casey's handling of Van Mungo, a Dodger pitcher. When that rugged individualist decided things weren't going as he wanted them to, he deserted the club in the West and returned alone to Brooklyn. Stengel issued no ultimatums; he told the big pitcher to follow his own inclinations. Mungo eventually got back into uniform, but there were those at Montague Street who thought Casey should have acted more forcefully in squashing this one-man mutiny.

When the season had ended, most sports writers and baseball men believed Casey had done well to keep his array of hooligans from falling into the cellar. He had stitched odds and ends together and won a number of ball games. He had devoted twenty-four hours a day to the welfare of the team, inspecting the unpromising prospects dredged up for him in the mornings at Ebbets Field, and attending banquets and smokers as the team's official representative in the evenings. He had kept the name of the Dodgers in print despite the overwhelming competition of the Yankees and Giants. He had worked hard to develop the skills of some of the more talented youngsters on the squad. And he was fired by the Dodgers' board of directors during the 1936 World Series.

7.

THE DODGER MANAGEMENT had again given the public a glimpse of the absurd tactics which passed for club policy. As his contract still had a year to run when he was banished for finishing seventh, Stengel, like his predecessor, Max Carey, was paid not to manage the Dodgers in 1937. His successor, Burleigh Grimes, had qualified for the job by masterminding Louisville to a seventh-place finish in the American Association.

Dodger president John Gorman's announcement that Stengel had been asked to do his thinking and clowning elsewhere was met by momentary indignation in the pages of the New York press. Sorry to see an old friend and, perhaps more to the point, a good source of copy, turn down his glass and move on, the sports writers fired a blast at the Brooklyn front office. They raked over the obvious. They pointed out that Stengel had done as well as could have been expected under the circumstances and, besides, that it was just plain bad business to pay two managers for one season's work. But the Yankees were putting on an impressive show of power in the World Series and Casey's name soon disappeared from the sports pages. When the Yanks had finished off the Giants in six games, the writers turned once again to Stengel and sent him on his way with one of the merriest base-ball wakes in memory.

The party, clotted with sentiment, was held at the Hotel New Yorker and 200 revelers paid their way in to honor the deposed manager of the Dodgers. At first it had been planned to restrict the list of guests to newspapermen, but a number of Yankee officials, including manager Joe McCarthy and George Weiss, then the director of the Yankee farm system, heard about the impromptu testimonial and asked if they could come, too. The flow of refreshments was steady, though probably not quite as steady as the flow of words from the guest of honor. Casey had a kind word for everybody and a comment on every subject. Seeing the Dodgers' first baseman, Buddy Hassett, at one of the tables, he remarked, "This is the first time a ballplayer ever paid to say anything *nice* about his manager."

His rambling speech, though free of any hint of bitterness toward his former employers, included at least one note of prophecy. "If I can do this well with a club that shoulda finished eighth," Casey said, "I know I'll be all right if I ever get a winner."

Casey divided his year of leisure between his home in California and the Texas oil fields. While he was managing the Dodgers he and several of his players had invested in oil wells and, though they had not made him a rich man, he took an active interest in them. But Stengel out of baseball was not a happy man. It was a long summer for him and he waited anxiously for an opening back into the big leagues. When he did return, it was not with the winner he had hoped for, but in those lean days a job in baseball was more important to him than victory.

Bob Quinn, who had been general manager of the Dodgers when Casey was appointed their manager in 1934, had left a year before Casey did to become president of the Boston Braves. The Braves, or the Bees as they were officially called from 1936 through 1940, were in a state almost as wretched as that of the Dodgers. In 1935 they had distinguished themselves as the most unimpressive team of modern times by losing 115 games. Under Bill McKechnie they had risen, perhaps buoyed by the law of averages, to sixth in 1936 and fifth in 1937, but it was a club built precariously around several aging pitchers. When McKechnie was lured by a better contract to Cincinnati at the end of the season, Quinn summoned Stengel to Boston. Casey agreed to manage the team and, in a display of faith in both baseball and the miserable Bees, he invested $43,000 of his own money in the club.

He lingered in Boston for six years. Readers with a taste for the dismal may turn elsewhere for a chronological account of the Bees' fortunes under Stengel. They finished fifth in 1938, seventh in each of the next four seasons and sixth in 1943.

It was at Boston that Casey first had a DiMaggio on his side. It was, however, the wrong DiMaggio. Vince was Joe's older brother, and while he resembled the great Yankee and could field and throw and hit the ball a long way, he could seldom get his bat around in time. Casey worked patiently with him in an effort to cut down on his strikeouts. When, at the end of the

1948 season, Vince had established an all-time major league record by striking out 134 times, Casey said to Quinn, "I helped him set the new record. Now maybe somebody else can make a hitter out of him."

One of Stengel's favorite players in those days was Max West. He was a big outfielder who could hit the ball out of sight and he won a number of games for the Bees. Stengel claims that few victories have given him more satisfaction than the one which West broke up with a home run off Johnny Vander Meer. Vandy, a lefthanded fastball pitcher, had just immortalized himself by pitching two consecutive no-hit, no-run games, one of them against the Bees. The next time the Bees came to Cincinnati Vander Meer was scheduled to pitch against them and a tremendous crowd was at Crosley Field to watch the new wonder boy.

"I rode out to the ball park with West," Stengel recalls, "and I says to him, 'How do you hit Vander Meer?' 'Great,' he tells me, 'absolutely great!' I tell him I'll bear that in mind. Well, the park's sold out. They got banners here and there from insurance companies and every kind of companies. Vander Meer had us beat going into the ninth and I says to West, 'Go up and hit one.' West hit one and we won it. I came to find out later on that West had got only about two hits off Vander Meer in his life. But he didn't tell me no lie. He hit Vander Meer great that night.

"Well, anyway, everybody in Cincinnati was mad at the way the game wound up. I got back to the hotel and they was standing around in bunches in the lobby and they was all beefing. I'd walk from one bunch to another and I'd say, 'Pardon me, I'm a stranger in town and I had to leave in the seventh inning. Can you tell me how the ball game come out tonight?' You never heard such squawking and moaning in your life. I went around like that until they finally recognized me, but I never had such a fine evening."

One of the brighter moments of Stengel's term in Boston arrived when Paul Waner joined the Bees. "Big Poison" had been one of the greatest of all hitters and, though he was now reaching the end of his career, he still handled a bat like a master. Casey could not help but like him, not only for his batting feats but also because he took his fun where he found it. Nobody ever restricted Waner to a curfew.

Casey loves to tell of the day when, sitting next to Waner on the bench during a Florida exhibition game, he told him to go up and hit one over the whiskey sign.

"Paul looks around at me and says, 'Which one?'

"I says, 'There's only one.'

" 'Where?' says Paul.

"I says, 'In right center. Can't you read it?'

"Waner tells me he can't. Here's one of the best hitters anybody ever saw and he can't read a sign in the outfield. I have to wear glasses to read the paper, but I can read the sign. So I ask him how he follows the ball.

"He looks at me and laughs and says, 'Mostly by ear, I guess.'

"I'm shocked and so I send him out to get glasses and he wears them during batting practice the next

92

day. Afterwards I ask him how does the ball look to him.

" 'It looks mighty small,' he says.

" 'How did it look before?' I ask him.

" 'Big as a grapefruit,' he says.

"So right then I tell him to throw the glasses away and hit at the grapefruit, even if it's a blurred grapefruit."

In 1943 Casey was engulfed in a sea of troubles. The war had deprived him of the few real ballplayers he had had to begin with; the other teams were similarly ravaged, but Casey's Bees were a feeble team in a poor league. His record in Brooklyn and Boston indicated that he was a second division manager, and most of his early supporters were beginning to desert him. "For the writers following the Bees," wrote Harold Kaese, "it was more fun losing with Stengel than with a hundred other managers they could name. Unfortunately, Boston fans did not have the benefit of Stengel's company."

Even some of the press, notably the caustic Dave Egan of the Boston *Record,* had lost their enthusiasm for Casey. Egan was particularly savage: "He's a great guy, except for those who work for him. He's a funny guy, too; always funny at somebody else's expense, and the somebody is usually within hearing distance. So he wound up with a sullen ball club and the majority of the players hated him. He ruined some of the young players, yet he always remained funny in his cruel and malicious way."

In the early spring, just before the season opened,

93

Stengel was walking across Kenmore Square in Boston. It was a miserable evening; a light drizzle was falling and the city was wrapped in fog. Stengel never saw the car that hit him. He was knocked to the pavement, his leg smashed, and several months in the hospital lay before him. Yet through those bleak days he remained alert and witty and still looked to the future with confidence.

When Edna, who was then caring for her ailing mother in California, was notified of the accident, she wired Casey that she was on her way East. He wired back: "Don't come unless you can set a broken leg."

Edna remained with her mother. Other wires poured into the hospital. One came from Frank Frisch, his old teammate on the Giants. It was addressed to Stengel, care of the psychopathic ward. Frisch needn't have strained himself for a gag; because of the war, the hospital was overcrowded and Casey had been lodged in the maternity ward.

The city of Boston was not unanimously sympathetic. In his newspaper column, Egan suggested that the driver who had run Stengel down be given a plaque as "the man who has done the most for Boston baseball in 1943."

Stengel finally returned to the Bees, but his presence had no therapeutic effect upon them. The Bees huffed and puffed through the remaining days of the season and finished in sixth place. At the end of the season the ball club was sold to three enterprising contractors who were dubbed "The Little Steam Shovels" in the Boston papers. They announced that

94

beginning in 1944, the club would again become the "Braves."

Stengel sensed that his days in Boston had come to an end. He was right. Lou Perini, one of The Little Steam Shovels and the man who was to move the Braves to Milwaukee ten years later, had invested money in the team before he and his two partners gained complete control of it. He had spent some time with the Bees during the 1943 spring training, and he had not been impressed by Stengel. Watching a game one afternoon, he saw Boston get a rally underway. Stengel sent a man up to bunt, the batter promptly bunted into a double play, and the rally collapsed. Perini went up to Stengel in the clubhouse after the game. "I don't know much about baseball, Casey," he said. "I wonder if you'd explain what happened out there during that rally."

Stengel launched into a monologue on the proper execution of the bunt and the way the wind was blowing and why the oysters hadn't been very good that winter. Because he did not know Stengel very well, Perini was utterly confused. "I wonder if you'd go over that again," Perini ventured.

Casey dutifully returned to his explanation, a rambling account that surpassed his previous one in irrelevance. Perini, not wanting to risk another interminable digression, let the matter drop, but he thought to himself, "This man can't really know very much about baseball if he isn't able to explain a simple play." He made up his mind that day that if he ever got control of the club he would hire a new manager.

After the sale of the club became official in January, 1944, Casey wrote to Bob Quinn: "Whenever a new group purchases control of a corporation they have the right to dictate the policy. And in order that there be no embarrassment on the part of this group I hereby tender my resignation."

Perini gratefully accepted it. The owner of the Braves, like an earlier Indian, had thrown a pearl away richer than all his tribe.

Stengel regained the $43,000 he had invested in the Braves, and big-league baseball thought it had seen the last of him. Disheartened, he toyed for a time with the idea of settling down in Glendale. His oil wells, which had suddenly come to life in 1941, promised him security and comfort for the rest of his days. Yet baseball was his life and, because victory is all-important in baseball, it grieved him that a forgetful posterity would remember him only as a clown who had managed bad ball clubs and concealed sparrows in his cap.

However, baseball soon called him back. In May, 1944, Charley Grimm gave up his job as the manager of the Milwaukee Brewers, then in the American Association, to join the Cubs. The Milwaukee club offered Casey the post. It wasn't the big leagues but it was baseball and Casey quickly accepted it. Unfortunately his reputation as a clown preceded him there. The directors of the club had decided on Stengel without consulting the president, Bill Veeck, who was then with the Marines in the Pacific. Veeck later told sportswriter Tom Meany that he was furious

Stengel as a New York Giant in 1922

United Press Photo

Casey as manager of the Brooklyn Dodgers, 1936

Casey Stengel is all seriousness as he confers with his new bosses, (left to right) George Weiss, Dan Topping, and Del Webb, after signing his first contract to manage the Yankees in October, 1948

Acme Photo

Yankee manager Stengel
(right) confers with pitching
coach Jim Turner during a
crucial moment of the 1952
World Series

United Press Photo

Yankee catcher Yogi Berra
watches as Stengel juggles the
ball at the mound while
awaiting a new pitcher

Acme Photo

The "Ol' Perfesser" holds a press session with sports writers in the dugout before a game with the Brooklyn Dodgers at Ebbets Field

United Press Photo

Manager Stengel with one of his brightest pupils, Mickey Mantle

Casey receives consolation from his wife, Edna, after the Yankees had lost the fifth 1957 World Series game to the Milwaukee Braves

United Press Photos

Stengel gives Milwaukee Braves manager Fred Haney a pat on the head in the Braves' dressing room after Milwaukee won the seventh and final game of the 1957 Series for the world championship

Casey Stengel gazes into his "crystal ball" to see what is in store for the Yankees in the future

when he learned of Stengel's appointment. He shared the prevailing opinion of Casey's ability. "He's mentally a second division manager," Veeck wrote to the directors. "He is entirely satisfied with a losing ball club as long as Stengel and his wit are appreciated. . . . If Stengel has an iron-clad contract and it will be expensive for us to cancel it, I guess that we're stuck with him. But he is not to be rehired next year."

Luckily Veeck was anchored to an atoll and Casey could go about the business of managing his team. It was a heady experience. The Brewers had a sound ball club and, for the first time since 1927, Casey found himself aboard a winner. The Brewers left the rest of the league behind them as they won the pennant. Word from the atoll, however, indicated that Veeck still hadn't changed his views; Casey, in his book, was still a clown. Stengel returned to Glendale, wrapped in glory but numbered among the unemployed.

At this time George Weiss again entered his life. The Yankees owned the Kansas City Blues in the American Association, and the manager's job there was open. Weiss, one of the few men in baseball who believed in Stengel's ability, signed him as the Blues' manager in January, 1945. Casey was pleased to receive an offer from the Yankee organization and intrigued by the prospect of managing in his old home town, but the Blues' predicament was all too familiar to him. They had finished last in 1945 and were appraised by oldtimers as the worst club ever to represent the city. The Yankee organization's opulence had been plundered by the war and Stengel had to struggle along with the collection of 4-F's and under-age players doled out to him. The Blues limped home in seventh place.

Stengel, now fifty-five years old, once more saw the handwriting on the wall. The one man in baseball who seemed to believe in him was Weiss, but George, as the Yankees' farm director, could keep Stengel only in minor league jobs. Casey and Edna talked it over in Glendale that fall and came to the conclusion that, though baseball meant so much to him, it would be pointless to spend his old age going to and fro in the earth and walking up and down in it as a minor league manager. California had been his home now for twenty years and, lacking a big-league job, he decided he would like to stay there. The job of managing Oakland was open. "It's close to home," he said to Edna, "and the travel ain't bad." Thus he became the manager of the Oakland Oaks in 1946.

The Pacific Coast League had long been a haven for fading ballplayers. "I still throw as hard as I used to," Lefty Gomez said at the end of his career, "but the trouble is the ball don't seem to go as fast." This league was infested with players plagued by similar problems. Those who read of Stengel's appointment to Oakland must have conceived the idea that this was also the legendary land where aged managers crept off to die.

Casey liked Oakland. He seemed particularly impressed by the Oakland Bay Bridge. "I like the idea of bridges," he said. "Everywhere I go they throw in a bridge as part of the service. Like at Brooklyn. Every manager wants to jump off a bridge sooner or later, and it is very nice for an old man to know he don't have to walk fifty miles to find one."

He needed neither bridges nor rusty razor blades at Oakland. The club was owned by Brick Laws, one of the minor leagues' most competent executives, and he provided far better material than Casey had been accustomed to; the Ol' Perfesser knew what to do with it. He finished second and fourth his first two seasons in Oakland, and won the pennant in 1948. Among the pitchers Casey had in 1946 were Frank Shea and Gene Bearden, both of whom were the property of the Yankees. Shea went to New York the next year and helped the Yankees win a world championship. Bearden was a lefthander whose fast ball, in Casey's opinion, was not good enough to get him by in the majors, and so he helped Gene perfect his knuckle ball. On Stengel's report that he wasn't fast, the Yankees sold Bearden to Cleveland, where he pitched the Indians to the world championship in 1948. Casey, however, was justified in the long run for Bearden blossomed only for that one season. He lost his touch immediately afterward and soon disappeared from the big leagues.

Among Casey's admirers at Oakland was Del Webb, a wealthy contractor who, with Dan Topping, owned the New York Yankees. Webb often visited Oakland on business and was an interested spectator at the Oaks' home games.

"I got to know Casey fairly well," Webb once said. "I was at a party in Oakland one night and Casey was among the guests. He was in rare form. He had us standing around with our mouths open, putting on one of the best shows I've ever seen—telling stories, hopping around the room, mimicking other people. I had an important business appointment early the next morning, so at about three a.m. I decided to duck out and catch a couple of hours sleep. When I left Casey was still holding forth.

"Well, I got my sleep—not much, but some—and then I staggered out and got a cab to take me to my appointment. We were going past a vacant lot and I looked out and there were a bunch of kids with bats and gloves gathered around an old gaffer who was giving them some instruction. I took another look just to make sure. The old gaffer was my friend Casey. I thought to myself then that if he really cared that much about baseball he must be a terrific manager."

Casey was making a good impression around the clock. In 1948 he had a collection of individualists, most of them veterans who had drifted to Oakland from the big leagues, but he forged them into a winning team. One of his older players there said, "If we won a doubleheader, Casey would come in the clubhouse and say, 'You fellas did pretty well today and it's up to me to buy you a three dollar dinner.' The next day he'd come in with a pocketful of bills and give each of us three bucks. In a playoff game that year we were getting beat, 9-2, and came back and won it, 23-15. It was the darnedest game you ever saw. Afterwards Casey said, 'Every man here rates a ten dollar dinner from the old man.' The next day he passed out ten bucks apiece to twenty-seven men from his own pocket. No wonder we played our heads off for him."

100

Having won Oakland's first pennant since 1921, Stengel was a hero in the city. The team's owners, Brick Laws and Joe Blumenfeld, staged a "Casey Stengel night" for him at the ball park and presented him with a new Cadillac. The gods were smiling on Stengel again and baseball men who had watched him at Oakland were changing their minds about him; perhaps he was something more than a clown after all.

He was to get an urgent phone call from New York a few days later which would mark the turning point of his life.

8.

"WELL, SIRS AND LADIES, the Yankees have now been mathematically eliminated from the 1949 pennant race. They eliminated themselves when they engaged Perfesser Casey Stengel to mismanage them for the next two years, and you may be sure that the perfesser will oblige to the best of his unique ability." This was the published reaction of Dave Egan, Stengel's long-time Boston sparring partner, to the announcement that Casey had been signed to manage the Yankees. While Mr. Egan represented an extremist wing of the opposition, it cannot be said that Casey's appointment to the biggest job of his life evoked wild cheers in any quarter. His unfortunate past as a big league manager and the ominous situation into which he had stepped combined to suppress the enthusiasm of even his warmest friends. Uneasy lay the crown upon this old gray head.

The summons had come suddenly while Stengel was leading his Oakland Oaks to victory in the postseason playoffs. The Yankees had been managed during 1947 and 1948 by Bucky Harris, a colorless but extremely likeable man with a sound baseball reputation. He had piloted a number of big league clubs in a career that spanned twenty-five years, finishing in the second division with the poor teams and win-

102

ning pennants with the good ones. In his first season
with the Yankees Bucky won the pennant and the
World Series and was acclaimed a hero in New York.
Then Dan Topping and Del Webb bought out Larry
MacPhail late in 1947 and George Weiss was made
the general manager. Ambitious and immensely industrious, Weiss wanted a pennant badly in his first
year of command. He was disappointed when the
1948 team, although in the race until the final weekend of the season, finished third. In a move that
shocked New York, Weiss fired Harris.

Weiss believed that Bucky had lost the pennant
through his failure to discipline a hard little core of
playboys who occupied key positions on the team.
Many sports writers and fans contended that Harris
had done remarkably well with his material. The writers also were irritated because Weiss had announced
Bucky's release while the Red Sox and Indians, having finished in a first-place tie, were preparing to meet
in a playoff game. Certain writers felt, and perhaps
correctly, that Weiss had tried to bury the sacking
of Harris under cover of the dramatic playoff battle.

On Sunday, October 10, Weiss called Stengel from
Cleveland, where the Yankee general manager was
attending the World Series between the Cleveland
Indians and the Boston Braves. "Casey," he said, "we
want you to fly to New York and meet us there tomorrow night. If you'd like to manage the Yankees,
the job's yours."

Casey, accompanied by Brick Laws, flew to New
York the next morning. He was promptly stowed out
of sight in a room at the Waldorf-Astoria; the grand

103

unveiling was not to take place until the following day. That night he was visited by Topping and Weiss, and he signed a two-year contract for $35,000 a year. He had become the fifteenth manager of the New York Yankees.

Most baseball clubs hold press conferences in their own headquarters. The Yankees, befitting their eminence, staged the introduction of Stengel to the press in one of New York's most sumptuous and exclusive restaurants, the "21" Club. The date was Tuesday, October 12, 1948, twenty-five years to the day since a defiant old New York Giant outfielder named Casey Stengel had hit a home run to beat the Yankees in the World Series, 1-0, and then had rubbed salt in their wounds by thumbing his nose at them.

There was no bravado in Casey now as he faced a small battalion of writers, photographers, and newsreel cameramen. If there were any present who hoped to see Casey play the buffoon they were disappointed. From the grim faces of the writers it was apparent that few expected either comedy or genius. All of them, young and old, were resentful of the treatment given Harris and they were convinced that Weiss and the Yankee owners had chosen Stengel to entertain the press while they set about rebuilding what appeared to be a fading ball club. What should have been a boisterously happy day for Stengel was clouded by tension and uncertainty.

To the writers Casey looked pale and his hair was grayer than they had remembered it. The paleness of his face was sharply emphasized by his dark blue

104

suit. He answered their questions soberly, in a low voice.

"Somebody asked a question about DiMaggio," Stengel said later, "and I said I didn't know DiMaggio. I could hear the hum in the background. When they talked about a pennant I could hear that hum again and I knew what they was talking about. They was saying, 'This bum managed nine years and never got into the first division.'"

Dan Topping delivered a small speech of welcome to Casey for the benefit of the newsreel cameras. Casey solemnly shook his hand and said in his confusion, "Thank you, Bob." Dan's brother, Bob, was a frequent subject of New York's gossip columns.

Perhaps the aspect of his new job which least disturbed Casey then was the charge that he had been hired because of his friendship with George Weiss. "Look," he pointed out to an old friend among the writers, "the Yankees represent a five-million-dollar business. They don't hand out jobs like this on a friendship basis."

Casey also believed that he could win the writers over to his side. However, his most anxious moments came when he looked at his new ball club. The Yankees still had some of the most famous names in baseball—DiMaggio, Phil Rizzuto, Tommy Henrich, Charley Keller—but age and injuries seemed to be stripping them of their once wonderful skills. The future of the ball club was not especially bright, and the Yankee empire, in the opinion of many baseball men, faced certain collapse unless Weiss immediately

105

began a vigorous rebuilding job. The Red Sox, with their devastating attack, seemed about to usurp the Yankees' position as the aristocrats of baseball.

First, the new manager had to get to know the coaching staff that had been assembled for him by Weiss. There was Jim Turner, an ex-pitcher who had hurled for Casey briefly in Boston and later was a rival manager in the Pacific Coast League; Casey made him his pitching coach. His other coaches were Frankie Crosetti and Bill Dickey, both great Yankee players of the past. It was a good staff and Casey realized that he could look to it for help, especially in the early days as he tried to feel his way around in a strange league.

It wasn't until he saw his team on the field at St. Petersburg that Stengel knew with what slender threads it was held together. He had inherited a major discipline problem from Harris. The ball club had assigned private detectives to the trails of several of the more carefree young Yankees in 1948, and Weiss had gathered a plump dossier on them. Only the plea of Stengel that he would like a chance to straighten some of them out had kept Weiss from making important trades during the winter. "You can tear a team apart in a couple of weeks," Casey said, "but it takes years to put one back together again."

One of Weiss' most consistent complaints the year before had been that the Yankees showed far more devotion to the task of picking a winner at the St. Petersburg dog track than to working themselves into shape on Huggins Field. The players could be found at the track every evening and, to the intense annoyance of Weiss, Harris was invariably there with them.

"I have no objections to seeing them at the track," Harris had said. "At least this way I know where they are."

For the first time in Yankee history, a midnight curfew was clamped on the players at spring training. Stengel also limited the players to one night a week at the dog track. After several weeks it was clear that Stengel was unhappy about the way in which his men were accepting the "new order." Many of the players were openly flouting the ban on the dog track; others were breaking all of Casey's regulations. Stengel let the players know he was aware of what was going on and threatened further restrictions in the future.

Far more disturbing to Stengel and Weiss was the physical condition of the team. There were a number of candidates for first base, but none was promising and it grew more apparent as time went on that Casey might have to have Tommy Henrich, his best outfielder aside from DiMaggio, play that position. George Stirnweiss, who had been the Yankees' second baseman, was slowing down in the field. Phil Rizzuto, the great little shortstop that Casey (or was it somebody else?) had chased out of Ebbets Field, was seriously handicapped by a shoulder injury. Third base was unsettled, with the veteran Billy Johnson and Bobby Brown, a good hitter but an uncertain fielder, battling for the job. The Yankees' unlikely-looking young catcher, Yogi Berra, could hit but he was an unbelievably awkward receiver. If Henrich moved in to play first base, Stengel's outfield problem would be further complicated. DiMaggio had undergone an operation for the removal of a bone spur from his left heel during the winter and the foot was alarmingly slow in healing. Joe was thirty-four, and obviously nearing the end of his career. Even closer to the end was the powerful Charley Keller, badly crippled by a slipped disc in his back. In addition to them, Stengel had Johnny Lindell, a reformed pitcher who had never quite lived up to his early promise as a hitter, and an unspectacular group of rookies.

The pitching staff was also badly riddled. Joe Page, "The Gay Reliever," had been out of shape in 1948, and most of the blame for losing the 1948 pennant which hadn't been heaped on Harris had been placed on him. Frank Shea, a starting pitcher, had also been out of shape, while Allie Reynolds, a hard-working young man for whom a fine future had been predicted, had stumbled through a disappointing season. Fred Sanford, another pitcher, had been bought from the St. Louis Browns for $100,000 during the winter and he was already displaying the form which would stamp him the biggest "mistake" Weiss has ever made.

Stengel knew that the best of his younger players was Berra, and he gave "Operation Yogi" high priority at St. Petersburg. The homely and powerfully built catcher was an extraordinarily gifted natural hitter and he had a good arm and quick reflexes. But his movements around the plate were as crude as his speech. Stengel assigned to Bill Dickey the task of

108

molding a creature of grace and beauty from this formless lump, and Yogi happily blossomed forth in the hands of his Arkansas Pygmalion.

"Dickey's teaching me all his experiences," Berra told the sports writers and then set about becoming the perfect student. Very soon they had stopped laughing at the squat little man.

Casey was content to let his older players—DiMaggio, Keller, Henrich and Rizzuto—work themselves into condition, and the Yankee manager was criticized by certain writers for this *laissez faire* policy toward them. "You can't let ballplayers pace themselves in the spring," was the way one of the writers summed up the opposition's viewpoint. "They'll just naturally let down, and the first thing you know the season will be open and these guys won't be ready."

The Ol' Perfesser shrugged off his critics. "Some people don't like the way I'm treating these players but I can't help that. Why, four fellas like this can carry a manager. What am I supposed to do? Push them?"

Perhaps some of the writers were annoyed with Stengel because he was not providing them with the comedy they had come to expect from him. Almost 59 now, Casey realized he was facing his one chance to go down in baseball history as something more than a clown. He saw nothing funny in the various tribulations which confronted him in his new job. For perhaps the only time in his life he was deadly serious about himself, his team, and all of his problems.

Casey's friends among the writers were genuinely

109

sorry for him. The old man, out in the cold so long, had been invited in after the fire had gone out. As he brought his crippled team north for the start of the season DiMaggio was being examined at Baltimore's Johns Hopkins Hospital. No one knew when Joe would be able to play again. When the Baseball Writers Association of America was polled by *The Sporting News* for its pennant selections, only six of the 206 writers thought that the Yankees would win. Cleveland, defending its world championship, was picked for first place and the Red Sox, managed now by Joe McCarthy and boasting a lineup which included the great Ted Williams, were placed second.

As the season began, the players had little confidence in their grim and, at times, apparently bewildered manager; and the fans and writers had little confidence in the team. Visions of sugar plums danced only in the head of Stengel. "I won't fail," he told a friend. "I never had so many good ballplayers."

Henrich opened the season playing in the outfield and batting in DiMaggio's old cleanup position. As he was to do so often during the 1949 season, Tommy came through with the hit necessary to keep Stengel's Opening Day at Yankee Stadium from being ruined. The Yanks were trailing, 2-1, going into the last of the ninth inning. With one man on, Henrich hit a long home run into the right center field bleachers and Casey won his American League debut, 3-2.

This sudden turn of the tide in the opening game gave the Yankees a tremendous lift. Casey, partly because of the injuries which soon began to attack his players in discouraging numbers and partly through his own incredible knack for having the right man in the right spot at the right time, began to shift his players in droves. When Stirnweiss was injured on the second day of the season, Casey put Coleman at second base. He alternated the left-hand-hitting Kryhoski and the right-hand-hitting Phillips at first base, according to the type of pitching the Yankees were facing. Rizzuto's shoulder trouble disappeared and he quickly became the league's outstanding shortstop. Elsewhere he shuttled players in and out of the lineup with a freedom no fan or writer could remember seeing before. Joe Page regained his ability to come in from the bullpen and suppress enemy rallies, and Stengel never hesitated to call him to the rescue. The Yankees seized first place and moved away from the rest of the league. Cleveland showed early in the race that it was not going to repeat its victory of 1948, but most baseball men waited for the Red Sox to combine their tremendous power with their strong pitching staff. It seemed only a matter of time before they would hit their stride, overtake the Yankees, and dominate what had so far been a lively pennant race.

But the Yankees kept winning. No one had ever seen a Yankee team like Stengel's. This wasn't a team of businessmen ballplayers in neat pin stripe uniforms; it did not have the superior class or win with the easy grace of its predecessors at the Stadium. It won the hard way, going into the dirt and wrestling for the ball game. It played with the exuberance of the old Gas House Gang.

Telling how Berra had stolen a base, Casey said,

"They don't think he can steal a base, but he can. Made this one on his face, of course, but he made it. He got the rest of the way around on a hit and when he come into the dugout he looked like he had a mask on, with the dirt all over his face."

All of the Yankees were coming into the dugout with dirt on their faces, and some had blood on them. The injuries piled up, but this was a courageous team, manned chiefly by players who had proved their courage on the battlefields of World War II—Hank Bauer, Jerry Coleman, Ralph Houk, Bob Porterfield, Tommy Byrne, Dick Kryhoski. "These kids have guts," Stengel would tell anyone who would listen to him. "We're liable to hustle ourselves right into the pennant."

Chanticleer is said to labor under the delusion that he is responsible for the rising of the sun. Casey had no delusions that he was hitting the home runs or catching the long fly balls, but he was playing the leading role in the Yankees' surge. He shuffled his lineup continuously, and he always had the right players on the field. At times he would sit quietly on the bench as one of his starting pitchers took an early pounding, then watch in satisfaction as the pitcher settled down, worked himself out of trouble, and went on to win the game. At other times he would remove his pitcher at the first sign of trouble, call in Joe Page or another of the relievers and watch his new hurler win the game. His moves were uncanny and often appeared to be prompted more by witchcraft than by "percentage."

By the middle of June, he had lost the magic touch

at first base. Both Kryhoski and Phillips stopped hitting. Casey did not hesitate. He called in Tommy Henrich from the outfield on June 23 and stationed him at first. "He can make the switch," Stengel told a writer. "Tommy's an old pro." And so another baseball expression was born; "old pro" is now a term as abused as the word "great" is on television, but it was meaningful when applied by Stengel to Henrich.

Stengel and the Yankees got another lift when DiMaggio returned to the lineup late in June. The Red Sox were moving up on them and the Yankees did not appear to have the manpower to hold them off. During a charity exhibition game with the Giants, DiMag tested his damaged foot and reported to Casey that he was ready to play. He had missed the season's first 65 games. The Yankees traveled to Boston for a three-game series with the Red Sox and they needed all the help they could get. The Sox were never an outstanding team on the road, but in their home park they were almost unbeatable.

DiMag limped off the bench to perform one of baseball's most memorable feats. He beat the awesome Red Sox into submission during three wonderful days of power hitting. His two-run homer won the opening game, 5-4; he came back the next day to lead the Yankee attack in a wild 9-7 game, slugging two homers and driving in four runs; and he completed the rout of the Sox on the final day by hitting a mighty home run into the light tower above the left field wall. It came with two men on and the Yankees won, 6-3.

Those who believed that Casey managed with a rabbit's foot rather than with a superior intellect were even more firmly convinced during the first game of the Yankees' July Fourth doubleheader against their arch-foes, the Red Sox. New York was leading, 3-2, in the first half of the ninth inning. The visiting Sox filled the bases with one out as Al Zarilla came to bat. Suddenly the sky darkened and a gust of wind darted in and whipped up a small dust storm over the infield. The elements had struck so swiftly that the umpires did not have time to hold up the game before Zarilla lined a "hit" to right field. Johnny Pesky, on third base, peered through the whirling dust and thought for a moment that the Yankees' rightfielder, Cliff Mapes, had caught the ball. Finally he dashed for home. Mapes, who had a fine arm, threw to Berra at the plate and, for a moment, Yogi was the only man in the ball park who knew exactly what had happened. He merely stepped on the plate, forcing Pesky and taking the "hit" away from Zarilla. Umpire Joe Paparella, like everybody else, believed another Boston player had scored ahead of Pesky and did not realize that the force was still on the runner. He signaled that Pesky was safe. It wasn't until he saw that the bases remained filled that Paparella knew Pesky's vision had been obstructed by the dust. The Red Sox had lost a run. A moment later the Yankees retired the final batter and walked off the field, under a clear sky and a bright sun, with an important victory. The Red Sox could have been excused for nervously scanning the heavens on succeeding days for further portents of divine intervention.

114

Weiss, not wanting the Yankees' pennant chances to rest solely on the vagaries of the weather or Casey's ingenuity, went into the market place and came up with a home-run-hitting first baseman named Johnny Mize. The Giants, rushing to oblivion that year, were building for the future under Leo Durocher and saw no place in their plans for the big, slow-moving slugger who was apparently nearing the end of his career. Weiss thought that the Yankees might need an occasional long hit as the season drew to a close and Mize was the best man available. He was bought for $25,000 on August 22.

Immediately after Mize arrived the team was struck by injuries in epidemic proportions. In a doubleheader at St. Louis on August 28, the Yankees were dealt two stunning blows. Mize threw out his shoulder in a play at first base, and Tommy Henrich, shifted to the outfield upon the arrival of Mize, crashed into the right field wall chasing a fly and fractured a small bone in his back. Mize was lost to the team for the rest of the season; Henrich did not return until September 23.

In another game at St. Louis in which they were hammering the Browns, 20-2, four New York batters were struck by balls thrown by Dick Starr and Karl Drews, two former Yankee pitchers. One of the pitches (which looked suspiciously like beanballs to Stengel's practiced eye) broke Berra's thumb. Casey was furious.

"Imagine two crows like that," he stormed. "They couldn't make good on this club and they haven't even made good with the Browns. They're getting their ears pinned back out there and so they try to get even this way."

The two offending pitchers pleaded "no control." Nevertheless, the Yankees were now riddled by injuries. The writers traveling with the team had to pack medical dictionaries along with their scorebooks if they were to write accurate accounts of the Yankees' fortunes. Still, to everyone's amazement, the team refused to fall back. Stengel used every trick he knew to keep a respectable lineup in action, and he maneuvered his pitchers with preposterous wizardry. For the first time in anyone's memory the Yankees had become national favorites. Fans outside of New York usually resent the Yankees' domination of baseball, but now the team was an underdog, battling for its life against a Boston team which had not suffered a single major injury all year. Even the writers with the team, men who like to present a veneer of blasé impartiality, lost their composure during ball games and rooted openly and fervently for Casey's tattered squad.

What appeared to be the crushing blow fell on September 18. DiMaggio was rushed to the hospital suffering from a virus. Badly weakened by the attack, he seemed finished for the season. The Red Sox kept gaining and, on September 26, having held the lead for 148 games, the Yankees dropped into second place. The writers who had cheered Casey on, now wrote glowing tributes to him, praising the ingenuity and leadership that had enabled him to keep what should have been a second division team on top for so long.

Neither Casey nor his team were ready to be counted out. A week of the schedule still remained to be played. Then there were only three games left, and many writers felt that the Yankees, one game behind, must win all of them to stay alive. They lost the first of the three to Philadelphia, but the Red Sox lost to Washington, and the two contenders prepared for their critical series at New York on the season's final weekend.

The attitude of coach Dickey, after the Yankees had lost to Philadelphia, was typical of the confidence the team had shown all year. "I still don't see where we're any worse off than when we started today's game," Dickey said. "We figured we had to win three games to win the pennant. Now all we need is two wins—against Boston over the weekend."

Stengel, though still a game behind, was confident as he came to grips with Manager Joe McCarthy's Red Sox in the Stadium on Saturday, October 1. DiMaggio, pale and weak after his battle with the flu, was back in the Yankee lineup. The Sox jumped off to a 4-0 lead in the early innings, and Casey put in his relief ace, Joe Page, in the fourth. As the lefthander stifled Boston with his fast ball, his teammates chipped away at the lead. By the eighth inning, the game was tied, 4-4. Then Johnny Lindell came to bat for the Yankees and hit a long home run into the seats in left field, Page got the Sox out in the ninth, and the two clubs were right back where they had

117

been on the opening day of the season—tied for first place.

One game to go, and Stengel knew that a whole season's work was wrapped up in it—in fact, the work of a lifetime. He was so very close now that he refused to believe his team could lose. He chose Vic Raschi to pitch against the Red Sox' veteran, Ellis Kinder.

In the first inning Phil Rizzuto, who had had a wonderful year, tripled and eventually scored. Then Raschi and Kinder battled tensely, brilliantly, down to the eighth inning. Here McCarthy, trailing by a run, had to put in a pinch-hitter for Kinder. Boston did not score in the top of that inning, and then the Yankees broke loose against Mel Parnell. Henrich crashed a home run to lead off and, after the Yanks had filled the bases, Coleman cleared them with a double to right. Leading 5-0 in the ninth, Raschi tired a little and Boston scored three runs. Finally, with two out and a runner on, Henrich glided back behind first and grabbed a pop fly for the third out, the ball game and the pennant. On the Yankee bench Dickey leaped from his seat in a fit of joy, banged his head on the dugout roof, and was carried off to the clubhouse, the team's 74th accident victim of the season.

It was a happy and satisfying moment for Stengel. The old man had confounded his critics, pleased and amazed his friends and convinced even those of little faith.

"Was it fun?" one of the writers asked in the clubhouse.

"It is now," Casey said grinning.

118

"But if you hadn't won it?"

"It would have been terrible. I'd liked to kill myself."

The World Series was an anticlimax. The ailing DiMaggio looked like a scarecrow, but even his presence was an inspiration to the other Yankees. Mize had recovered sufficiently to be ready to pinch-hit. Henrich seemed sound again, Berra was behind the plate and Rizzuto was at the peak of his career. A Yankee team that had seen DiMaggio, Henrich and Berra together in the lineup only 15 times in a 154-game season was supremely confident now that they were all as close to being able-bodied as anyone could expect. The Dodgers had won in the National League, also on the final day, but they looked less imposing to the Yankees than the powerful Red Sox had been.

The Yankees won in five games. Reynolds and Don Newcombe staged a pitching duel in the first and the Yanks won, 1-0, when Henrich hit a home run in the bottom of the ninth. After Raschi lost to Preacher Roe, 1-0, in the second game, the Yanks beat the Dodgers at Ebbets Field, 4-3; Mize, coming up as a pinch-hitter, drove in two runs with a ninth-inning single. It was easy the rest of the way. They pounded Newcombe for a 6-4 victory the next day and then wound up the Series at Brooklyn in the fifth game, winning 10-6.

"Give the credit to the players," Stengel said afterward. "I couldn't have won it with football players."

There was a victory party at the Biltmore Hotel that night. All of the players and their wives and

119

many friends of the ball club were there and suddenly the band broke into "Yankee Doodle Dandy" and they led Stengel down the aisle. He had on a dark blue suit and a white shirt, and his face was pale and tired, just as it had been almost a year before when he had stood before the press at "21" Club. But there was also on his face now a look which expressed how much victory meant to a man who had sought it for so many years and had finally caught up to it when he was almost 60. The guests stood and applauded Casey as he and Edna walked past the crowded tables, and there was no doubt where they thought the credit for victory belonged.

It was one of the great managing jobs of all time. It was also, as one guest was to say that night, "Casey's greatest gag."

9.

THUS BEGAN the most durable reign any team, or any one man, has enjoyed in baseball. The 1949 triumph was the first of five straight world championships captured by Stengel and his ball club, surpassing by one the achievement of Joe McCarthy's Yankees of 1936-39. Casey's team did not have the tremendous power that characterized Yankee teams in previous years, but he had three other assets even more favorable to a long stretch of success. In Allie Reynolds, Vic Raschi, and Eddie Lopat he had a trio of incomparable "clutch" pitchers, men who invariably won the important games during the season and in a World Series. Because of his capacity for shuffling players in and out of the lineup in bewildering numbers he soon developed the most versatile 25-man squad in the history of the game; and, of course, he retained his own elastic habits of mind that enabled him to vary his strategy according to the changes in the modern game and the players he had at his command. Stengel had become the greatest figure in baseball.

Having so recently stepped from the role of clown to one of baseball eminence, he was acutely aware of the irony in his position. He was elected almost unanimously the "Manager of the Year." The season

121

before, Billy Meyer, a minor league manager most of his life, had been given that award for leading the Pirates to a fourth-place finish. His club dropped to sixth in 1949, and Meyer's job was in jeopardy. Seeing him at the major league meetings during the winter, Stengel walked over and stuck out his hand. "Ain't it funny, Billy," he said, "how all of a sudden I got so smart and you got so dumb?"

1950 began on a genuinely bewildering note. Arthur Patterson, then the Yankees' publicity man, tells the story.

"Casey had had a very tough winter," Patterson recalls, "because everybody in southern California wanted him to come to the banquets they were tossing. He should have gone back to Glendale for a rest, but as it was he showed up at St. Petersburg in the spring looking more tired than he'd been after the World Series. The sponsors of the Yankees' radio and television broadcasts were throwing a series of parties down there and of course Casey was the center of attraction at all of them. They wouldn't let him go to bed at night. One day after spring training started, Dr. Sidney Gaynor, who was the team's physician, came over to me.

" 'You know,' he said, 'I think something's wrong with Stengel. He's talking funny.'

"I grinned at Gaynor. 'Doc,' I said, 'you just don't know Casey.'

" 'Oh, I know all about that,' he said. 'But this is different. I think he's suffering from nervous exhaustion.'

"So we went and got Weiss and took a look at Casey

and it turned out that he was so worn out from the round of parties and banquets that he was almost in a daze. Gaynor told him to take it easy for a few days, just sort of sit in the sun and get plenty of sleep. We decided not to tell anybody else about it because when something like this gets in print it always sounds a lot worse than it really is. Well, Casey wasn't himself for a couple of days, but he always talks like he's just coming out of ether anyway, so nobody ever caught on."

With one title already to his credit, Stengel found it even harder to stay on top than it had been getting there. During that season he spoke to sportswriter Bill Heinz of the problems that confronted any manager trying to string two pennants together:

"It's tougher the year after you win than it is the year you win," he said. "It has to be. You start out rating everybody off what they did for you the year before, and everybody doesn't do the same."

There were few who believed that Stengel would repeat. 1949 had been a miracle, a "gag"; now class would tell. Only 38 of 194 writers picked the Yankees to win in *The Sporting News* poll. Henrich was coming to the end of his career, and DiMaggio was off to a slow start, a handicap which he later corrected with a brilliant finish. Casey now had a young lefthander named Whitey Ford to go with his veteran pitchers, and the ineffable Berra, now just coming into his own.

For the moment, however, Berra remained Casey's most vexing problem. "Yogi knows every hitter in the league, except himself," he once said. "He is the only one that don't know what a good hitter he is. But all the pitchers know. Every pitcher in the league knows he wants to hit at everything, and don't like to take a pitch, even if it is away out here. Ever notice him when he gets a 'take ' sign? He makes a face like this."

Casey screwed up his face until his witnesses would have sworn they had seen the frustrated Mr. Berra in the act of leering. Then Casey went into a pantomime of Yogi's batting stance, peering back at an imaginary pitcher, following the flight of the ball, tensing, and letting the ball go by.

Then he straightened up. "Gentlemen," he said, wagging his head, "if I could get Mr. Berra to do that, he would lead the league."

But despite Yogi's passion for swinging at anything thrown in his direction, he was becoming one of the league's most dangerous hitters. His bat was sorely needed in the Yankee lineup. The rebuilding job was going on at the Stadium and Casey had to make another patchwork team do. Joe Page had slipped, and would henceforth be of little use to the Yanks. Mize, off to a slow start, was optioned in May to the Yankee farm team at Kansas City. The Red Sox were heavy betting favorites to win the pennant, but Detroit proved surprisingly strong, grabbed the lead, and for a while looked as if they were not going to let go of it.

Stengel schemed feverishly to keep his strongest unit on the field, and the team got better as the summer waned. DiMaggio was again a great ballplayer. Rizzuto was scampering through his best year. Mize, back from Kansas City in June and bulging with new life, became invaluable to Casey's concep-

124

tion of baseball. Used regularly, Mize added a dangerous bat to the lineup. Held out of the starting lineup, he was the prince of pinch-hitters, a *deus ex machina* which Stengel could lower into the game at a critical moment, knowing that the enormous slugger could make everything right with one swipe of his bat.

"Mize could do it for you three ways," Casey once said admiringly of his pinch-hitter. "He could get the base hit, he could get the long fly, and he could stick it in the seats."

Traditionally a team's best pinch-hitter was held out until the late innings, since managers had always believed any turning point in a game would come then. Stengel preferred to scrap tradition. He would throw Mize into the game if he saw a chance to break it up in the early innings. He knew that a big hit then could blow the game wide open, removing the necessity for a "turning point" later on. With men on bases Casey could send Mize up to bat for a weak-hitting infielder in the third or fourth inning, get the hit that would put the game out of reach for the other team, and still have another strong defensive infielder ready to replace the one he had removed. Such tactics helped to revolutionize the modern game.

Now that Stengel had proved he could win in the big leagues, the writers watched a change come over him. The comic touch they had missed in 1949 was again bubbling to the surface. He could laugh at himself again, could see the humor in what, the year before, had seemed to him like life-and-death situations. Everyone welcomed the return of "the old Stengel"

—everyone except the American League umpires, that is. Few of them relished the old man's sarcasm.

"If that Stengel keeps 'fainting' in the dugout every time I call a strike on one of his players," an umpire said, "I'm going to report him to the league."

When he heard of the umpire's complaint, Stengel had a quick reply. "If he keeps calling strikes like he's been doing, he won't have to report me. My team will lose the pennant and I'll be out of a job."

Having fared well with one National League cast-off, the Yankees went scavenging in the league again in 1950 and came up with another first baseman, Johnny Hopp. Hopp took the place of the disabled Henrich on the roster, and while he did not have the brute power of Mize, he was more agile at first base. Meanwhile the team moved closer to the leading Tigers. On September 16, Ford pitched them to an 8-1 victory over Detroit and the Yankees took over first place. They clinched the pennant on September 29, two days before the end of the season.

The World Series that year was the easiest Stengel would ever be likely to know. The Philadelphia Phillies were young, spirited, and had a good pitching staff, but their hitters were weak and inexperienced. Raschi, who had won 21 games during the season, was the manager's choice to pitch the opening game. Mize played first base. With the Yankees leading, 1-0, in the ninth inning, Casey took out Mize and replaced him with Hopp. The more agile first baseman promptly made a great play to rob Richie Ashburn of an extra base hit that might have tied the score.

The Yankees continued to stifle the Phillies' at-

126

tack. After Raschi had shut them out in the opener, Reynolds beat them, 2-1, on DiMaggio's tenth inning home run, and Coleman played brilliantly as they swept the third game, 3-2. Ford started the final game and was leading, 5-0, in the ninth inning. Then the Yankees' leftfielder, Gene Woodling, dropped an easy fly that let two runs score. Here Stengel came to the top of the dugout steps and performed a pantomime in front of 65,000 fans, staggering around under an imaginary fly ball. Then he brought in Reynolds to relieve Ford. As he walked off the field with Whitey, the crowd, wanting to see the young pitcher finish the game, booed Stengel lustily.

Reynolds struck out Stan Lopata on three pitches to end the game and the Series. In the clubhouse afterwards, the writers asked Ford if, having pitched that far, he was disappointed by Stengel's change. Whitey graciously, or perhaps wisely, refused to criticize his manager. "I was losing my stuff," he explained, "and besides, Stengel hasn't made a mistake all year."

Other players were not as quick to excuse the manager's public humiliation of Woodling. It was a sore that would fester in many breasts, including Woodling's, for a long time.

With two world championships to his credit, Stengel had securely established himself in the Yankee organization. During the winter he signed a two-year contract for $65,000 a year; the Yankees also awarded Casey a "bonus" for winning the pennant. Now for the first time Stengel could look past what had always before been the precarious moment to a future in which he would be the beneficiary of an endless source of talented young players. He asked George Weiss to establish a "rookie school" at which he would serve as the head "perfesser." All of the promising players in the Yankees' minor league organization would be assembled at this school, which would operate just before spring training opened. There Stengel and his staff would stress the fundamentals of the game, examine the players for obvious faults and try to correct them, determine which position each was best suited to play, and get an idea of each player's development and what his chances were to make the Yankee team.

The school was an unqualified success, and the idea has been widely copied by other big league teams. More important, it has provided the Yankees with the stream of talent that Stengel had asked for. An extraordinary percentage of the twenty-eight minor league players who matriculated at the school in Phoenix, Arizona, during the winter of 1951 went on to play in the major leagues. Among them were Gil McDougald, Tom Morgan, Gus Triandos, Tom Sturdivant, Jackie Jensen, Bob Cerv, Bill Renna, Bill Skowron, Clint Courtney, Bob Wiesler, Kal Segrist, Jim Brideweser, Gerry Snyder, Lou Berberet— and a muscular young man from Commerce, Oklahoma, named Mickey Mantle.

The arrival of Mantle made the 1951 spring training period the most exciting in years. The Yankees trained at Phoenix that year and Mantle was a legend before a ball was thrown or a muscle pulled. The reports from the rookie school indicated that this nineteen-year-old blond could hit the ball farther than Babe Ruth and run faster than Ty Cobb; what added spice to the legend was Mantle's ability to hit from *either* side of the plate. When training started, writers had assembled from all over the country to view this prodigy. To everyone's astonishment and delight Mickey *did* perform all the feats the publicity men said he could. Here was superman incarnate—a player, they said, destined to be the greatest ever. He had about him the glamour which only remoteness can give to a hero; he had never been seen by the public and his flaws had not tarnished the legend of perfection.

Every baseball fan in the country was asking the same question. Was Mickey Mantle as good as they said he was? Stengel was certain that if he wasn't a superman he was surely good enough to help the Yankees win their third straight pennant. The manager of the Yankees, grimly determined to retain the grip he now held on the championship, preferred some of the inexperienced but potentially great young players he had seen at the rookie school to the collection of veterans and part-time players he now had on the Yankee roster. He talked enthusiastically of Mantle's ability. When Mickey was called out one day on a close play at third base, a writer asked Stengel if he believed the umpire had missed the play.

"I don't know whether he was out or not," Casey said, "but I can see why the umpire thought he was. That kid got from first to third so fast they must have thought he ran across the pitcher's box."

A dispute arose between George Weiss and Stengel

when the manager announced he wanted not only Mantle, but McDougald, Jensen and Morgan, as well. Weiss believed most of the young players needed another year of minor league experience. Stengel had his way, and the Yankees arrived in New York for the new season.

A pre-season exhibition game had been scheduled with the Dodgers at Ebbets Field. Casey, who had played there when that park was opened in 1913, took Mantle out early in the morning to teach him to play the tricky wall in right field—the same wall he had learned to play by bouncing fuzzy old balls against it.

"I got him out there," the manager recalled, "and told him I knew all about the wall because I had played it myself. The kid looked at me like he was astonished. I guess he thought I was born 58 years old and right away became the manager of the Yankees."

On opening day the sports writers who had not been with the team in Phoenix flocked around Stengel to ask him about Mantle. Casey was desperately anxious for the boy to make the team now, and he was beginning to feel that all the publicity being lavished on him would bewilder and eventually hurt him. "He was pretty awkward playing the outfield this spring," he told the writers. "He was a shortstop in the minors and the first time we put him in the outfield and hit a fly ball to him it stuck right on top of his head."

This was an excusable exaggeration. The ball had bounced off Mantle's shoulder, but Stengel was trying to temper the original excessive publicity for Mickey. This was difficult for him, because he was fascinated by the boy's speed and power. Talking to the writers one day, he observed, "They say Tris Speaker used to outrun the ball, which I guess he did, but Speaker was outrunning the dead ball. This kid outruns the live ball."

Mantle began the year in right field because DiMaggio, now playing his final season, had been the Yankee centerfielder since 1936 and was, of course, the best of his time. The writers traveling with the team caught Stengel's enthusiasm and devoted most of their stories to the boy wonder. One day Mantle went hitless and misplayed a ball in the outfield. Afterward a visiting columnist asked Casey what had happened.

"My writers had an off day," the manager said.

The Yankees, their lineup studded with rookies, pulled away to an early lead, and it appeared for a time that they might win this one easily. Then, as Henrich remarked, "The White Sox decided to come along for the ride." Right behind Chicago were the Red Sox and Indians, both making threatening noises. When the Yankees arrived in Chicago for an important series their manager was the old Stengel who had winked, joked and grimaced around the National League as the manager of the Dodgers and the Bees.

"Look at these kids I'm playing," he said to a reporter as he made out his lineup. "In some states where they have strict labor laws I'd have to carry their parents with them so I wouldn't go to jail."

Then, turning to John Carmichael and several other Chicago writers, he grinned and rubbed his chin. "But putting them in there against the White Sox,

131

you know, I make a friendly atmosphere in Chicago. The Sox think to themselves, 'Mighty nice of Ol' Case to start his third and fourth teams against us.' Then they turn around and beat Boston and Cleveland for our benefit."

To Stengel's dismay, all of his "juveniles" came through handsomely except the one who "couldn't miss"—Mantle. Mickey hit a ball out of sight occasionally, but the good pitchers preyed on his inexperience. Lifted to glory before his time by the writers, then abruptly pulled down by American League pitchers, the boy was bewildered and discouraged. Stengel had no choice but to send him to Kansas City for a breathing spell. So certain was he of Mantle's greatness that he believed the husky young outfielder would rejoin the Yankees in a few weeks. Optioned to the Blues on July 16, Mickey was recalled on August 20, in time for the stretch drive.

Almost as upsetting to Casey as the failure of his *wunderkind* was a kidney stone which periodically sent him to his bed. "It's just a small one," he told the writers. "Must have picked it up when I was playing Class B ball."

But the ailment, coupled with the manager's advancing years (he was 61 that summer) stirred frequent rumors of his retirement. These stories, which appeared regularly during his first five or six years with the Yankees, reached their peak that fall when Bill Corum exclusively revealed in the New York *Journal-American* that Stengel would resign that winter. According to Corum's story, the Yankees faced

132

a complete rebuilding and Stengel felt he was too old for the job. He would be succeeded by his coach, Frank Crosetti.

This story proved to be as wrong as the countless and less exclusive rumors heard by anyone who kept his ear to the ground. Like the train usually heard when one keeps an ear to the railroad tracks, Casey's retirement was a long way off. As far as he was concerned, the kidney stone was a better subject for a story. He made its passing late that summer the subject of one of his most lurid, spine-tingling and gruesomely hilarious pantomimes for the entertainment of the writers. Having passed the stone and recovered Mantle, he felt ten years younger.

The Indians challenged the Yankees in September, but the Yanks swept a two-game set from them at the Stadium in the middle of the month. They beat Bob Feller, 5-1, in the first game, and won the second, 2-1, when Rizzuto's artful squeeze bunt scored DiMaggio in the bottom of the ninth inning. Then once again the Yankees clinched the flag two days from the end of the season, when they met Boston in a doubleheader. As the ninth inning of the opening game began, Reynolds had in his grasp his second no-hitter of the year.

"Get 'em this inning, Allie," Stengel said, "and I'll give you the rest of the season off."

Reynolds, bearing down, got the first two hitters out and forced Ted Williams to hit a high pop foul to Berra. To Allie's dismay, Yogi dropped it. Reynolds went right back to work and Williams hit another pop

133

foul. The abashed Mr. Berra held this one. Vic Raschi won the second game and Stengel had his third straight flag.

The 1951 World Series was the most bitter that Stengel had yet seen as a Yankee. The Giants, a sound, resourceful team, managed by the aggressive Leo Durocher and afire with the spirit that had driven them to their celebrated "miracle" pennant, thumped the Yankees in two of the first three games. The Yankees appeared bewildered, while the Giants, riding on the momentum of their furious pennant surge, stirred their followers to dreams of glory. Before the fourth game, which was played at the Polo Grounds, the Yankee players dressed slowly and a handful of them started out the clubhouse door for the long walk across the outfield. Suddenly Crosetti, a smart and intense baseball man known for his reticence, spoke up.

"Hold it, you guys," he called. "When we go out of here, we'll look like a ball club. We'll all go together."

The other players, startled for a moment, quickly dressed and waited for an order to leave the clubhouse. Stengel noticed that DiMaggio, the elder statesman, had just been handed the cup of coffee over which he traditionally lingered before going on the field. Casey always felt that Joe's greatness allowed him at least the privilege of arriving there last.

Taking over from Crosetti now, the manager said, "All right, let's get out there. Joe, you can come later."

DiMaggio put down his cup and stood up. "I'm going out with everybody else," he said quietly.

134

The Yankees proudly walked across the field, apparently unmoved by the jeers of the hostile fans, sailed into the Giants with a zest they had previously lacked, and did not lose another game. The only bizarre touch left was Stengel's strategy in the final game. The Giants, trailing in the ninth inning, filled the bases with nobody out. They had their right-handed power hitters, Monte Irvin and Bobby Thomson, coming up. The conventional move would have been to counter with a strong-armed righthanded pitcher. Instead Stengel called in an obscure left-hander named Bob Kuzava. Irvin, Thomson and Sal Yvars, a righthanded pinch-hitter, all hit the ball hard, but right at Yankee outfielders, and Stengel had won his third straight world championship. Genius had never looked with less reverence upon tradition.

There were many changes in the spring of 1952. DiMaggio had retired over the winter, following Henrich and Keller into exile. Coleman, Morgan and Brown were in the service. Mantle was on hand, but favoring a knee which had been operated on after the 1951 World Series. Just coming into his own as a star was Billy Martin, a loud, saucy infielder who had played for Stengel briefly at Oakland, and of whom the manager was very fond. There was in this slender boy the aggressiveness and resourcefulness which Casey has always admired. Billy had joined the club late in 1950, but had so far seen little action. Now Stengel felt he was ready, but to the old man's disgust, Martin broke a bone in his leg, not in the line of duty, but while sliding for a television cameraman. He was lost to the club for the early part of the season.

135

If there were changes in the makeup of the Yankees, there was no change in the experts' pre-season opinions of their prospects. Again, less than half of the voting writers thought they could retain their championship, and looked to Boston or Cleveland as the eventual winner. The fans, less knowledgeable, perhaps, but apparently awed by Stengel's magic and the Yankees' skill, generally were resigned to another New York triumph. The bookies altered their odds accordingly.

The Yankees moved sluggishly through the early months of the race. A few barbs were hurled at the team in the papers, and Stengel was annoyed. "I have heard," he said in the dugout one day, "that this isn't a very good ball club, or else it does not have any guts. It's too bad I had to use it in the World Series last year."

Soon Martin was back in the lineup and the team came to life. Billy was usually in trouble on the field, fighting the other team with his mouth and his fists, as well as with bat and glove. One day he and Jim Piersall of the Red Sox rolled in the dirt, punching and mauling each other. Stengel, who never restricted Billy's use of his tongue, did not like to see him risk banishment from a game because of a fight. "If I'd wanted a fighter," he told Martin, "I would have hired Rocky Marciano."

Cleveland, led for the second year in a row by three twenty-game winning pitchers, fought the Yankees bitterly for the lead. The Yanks moved into first place to stay on August 23, when Raschi outpitched Cleveland's Early Wynn, 1-0. But they did not take command of the race as Stengel believed they should have. The Indians were still close behind when, on September 5, the Yankees lost to Philadelphia. That night the team left by train for Washington. Stengel, tired and morose, ate in the dining car with his coaching staff. It was the only silent table in the car. Around him the players were passing the time with a lively game of "Twenty Questions," shouting in delight when one of them was stumped, laughing hilariously at a silly answer. Stengel's face grew darker as the noise increased.

Finally he stood up. "I got a question to ask you fellas," he growled. "Who won today's game?"

Then he withered them with a violent harangue. Moments later a long file of silent and red-faced ballplayers trooped back through the train, and Casey was left to grumble alone over his cold coffee.

The Yankees, jolted from their complacency, won fifteen of their next eighteen games and clinched the pennant.

The 1952 World Series was one of the most exciting ever played, and the Yankees won again, this time in seven games. They met what was probably the finest of all Brooklyn teams, but Reynolds, Raschi and Lopat, aided by some astounding slugging by the venerable Mize, eventually overwhelmed the Dodgers. Yet, in this Series of great names and heroic individual performances, it was the obscure Bob Kuzava, almost forgotten since his appearance a full year before, on whom Casey called to lock up the final game. Stengel brought him in to pitch to the lefthanded-hitting Duke Snider when the Dodgers threatened

137

in the seventh inning. When Kuzava retired Snider on a pop fly the crowd expected Stengel to follow with a righthanded pitcher to face Jackie Robinson. But Stengel left Kuzava to his own devices, and Bob pitched himself out of the inning. Then, though the Dodgers were supposed to devour any unfortunate lefthander found lurking at Ebbets Field, Kuzava remained in the game and throttled them in the last two innings.

Casey, of course, had a ready answer for all those with raised eyebrows who attended his post-game interview. "The Dodgers don't see lefthanders much any more," he explained. "I figured by the time they got used to this fella, the game would be over and we'd be back in the clubhouse."

The next year, 1953, Casey broke the record with five straight world championships—a chain of infinite allure, for which the greatest teams and the greatest managers before him had reached, and failed to grasp. In the spring even the "experts" believed in Stengel and his ball club. They confirmed the opinion of the fans, the bookmakers, and that of the disinterested observer, who felt that the Yankees couldn't miss. Stengel was sorely tried in attempting to suppress his optimism. "I really got something to worry about this year," he said. "They tell me we can't miss going for this number five."

On the first day of spring training he called several writers aside. "Wanna hear me make my first clubhouse speech of the year?" And then, turning to the players: "Men, it's now 10:28 a.m. In two minutes we're going out that door single file. The movie men are all set up and I don't want a man to miss that camera. If you don't think he got a good shot as you went by, go back to the end of the line and come past again. Rizzuto goes first after me 'cause he's the captain. I want Martin to come next 'cause he helped me manage the team a lot last year. Made some suggestions which I vetoed and made me look good."

Casey was even optimistic about Mantle, whose progress to the greatness so often predicted for him was, at times, frustratingly halting. "This year," Stengel announced to the writers, "if Mantle could play great I know I'd be better than last year. Look at the way he can hit lefthanded to left field and right field and righthanded to right field and left field and he's fast on his feet for a baserunner and a strong fella if he can improve his play."

Having divested himself of those weighty sentiments, the manager of the Yankees led his team to the strongest start of his tenure there. They moved into first place early in May and did not relinquish it the remainder of the season. Beginning on May 27, they won eighteen straight games, including a fourteen-game sweep through the West. Casey, who would like to win each of every season's 154 games, was almost beginning to enjoy himself. Then, on July 21, the Yankees abruptly plunged into the most frightening slump of Stengel's reign. They lost nine in a row. Stengel had ridden out slumps with the worst of them; nobody knows more about the anatomy of a losing ball club than a man who had managed Brooklyn and Boston during the Thirties. But this was different. That the Yankees had already proved themselves the best in the league made it all the more galling to the old man, for he is most frantic when he senses that his team is losing its grip on a game or a pennant race in which it has taken the lead.

As loss was piled on loss, the manager lapsed into sullen silence. Only occasionally did he rise out of it, and then only to express his displeasure and return immediately to his own gloomy thoughts. Even his favorite recreation, the reading of the sports pages, became a joyless experience as he saw their unfavorable accounts of the Yankees' misfortunes. When someone summoned the temerity to ask him what had gone wrong, he waved his hand impatiently.

"Everything is bad," he said. "Our batting, our pitching, our fielding, our managing. And judging by what I read in the papers the Yankee writers is in a slump, too."

The Yankees lost their ninth straight in Boston. After the game, Stengel, his chin jutting forward, clumped into the clubhouse. Right behind him came a delegation of Yankee writers, pencils poised to record the master's spicy comments. Stengel whirled and slammed the clubhouse door with such violence that it nearly squashed the nose of Daniel M. Daniel, the dean of Yankee writers.

Now there were wounded feelings on both sides. Stengel, in barring the writers from his clubhouse, had violated what they considered the rights of the press. He had raised his own iron curtain, and rudely, too. Fortunately, the calm head that sits upon the shoulders of Mr. Daniel prevailed. When the Yankees finally broke out of their slump the next day, Daniel

140

approached the manager in a spirit of good will and Casey, perhaps appeased more by victory than by an olive branch, made his peace with the press.

The Yankees had weathered their only major crisis of the season. From there on they romped to the easiest of the five pennants, finishing 8½ games ahead of the fading Indians. The Dodgers, while strong, did not provide them with the fierce battle of the previous October. With the Series tied at two games apiece, Mantle walloped a grand slam home run at Ebbets Field to blow open the fifth game, and the Yankees returned to the Stadium needing only one more victory to clinch their fifth straight championship. With his team leading 3-1 in the eighth inning, Stengel detected that Ford, his starting pitcher, was tiring. To the amazement of the crowd, he removed him and brought in Reynolds. For a precarious moment it appeared that Casey had generously tossed a juicy morsel to his critics. The Dodgers' Carl Furillo hit a two-run homer off Reynolds to tie the game in the top of the ninth. But Stengel was taken off the hook in the bottom of that inning when his pet, Martin, broke up the game with a single through the middle of the diamond.

The sparrow and the grapefruit will be remembered for a long time, but so will those five straight world championships. No other manager had ever left so imposing a monument.

10.

DEFEAT CAME to Stengel like a thief in the night.

For weeks during the 1954 season there lay on the desk in his office at Yankee Stadium a copy of a novel by Douglass Wallop. Called *The Year* THE *Yankees Lost* THE *Pennant,* it had been published not long before and was soon to be made into the musical comedy, *Damn Yankee.* Casey seldom reads a book, but for some reason he did not sweep this ominous portent off his desk. A writer pointed out the unpleasant overtones.

"Somebody sent it to me," Stengel muttered, obviously preoccupied with matters that struck closer to home than literature. "It's just fiction. It ain't a true story."

He had predicted a sixth straight championship, sometimes directly, sometimes in Stengelese, ever since clinching the pennant the year before. Immediately after his team had mathematically eliminated Cleveland on September 14, 1953, he had called "his" sports writers into the clubhouse and laid claim to the next season's flag, as well as to the one he had already wrapped up. "My team is just growing into greatness," he had said, "and it will win again."

It is seldom that Casey openly predicts a Yankee

142

victory. But that winter he indicated by a unique semaphore of winks and smirks and grimaces that he was uncommonly pleased with his players and almost desolate at the thought of what the coming season held in store for the rest of the American League. Fans around the country were already resigned to what they believed would be another in an endless chain of Yankee triumphs. Resigned, yes, but not ecstatic at the prospect. Many, having hoped and prayed for Casey's battered heroes in 1949, were now in the position of drought-ridden farmers who had beseeched an attentive deity for rain. Standing in the deluge their prayers had brought, they looked reproachfully up at the heavens and spluttered, "We prayed for rain, but *this* is ridiculous!"

It is ironic that the Yankees should lose a pennant while winning 103 games—the highest total a big league team has ever captured under Stengel. The Indians, though they had little speed and a mediocre defense, had a certain amount of power and a magnificent pitching staff. On the other hand, the staff on which Stengel had leaned for five seasons—headed by Reynolds, Raschi and Lopat—had broken down. Cleveland, picking chiefly on the second division clubs (who troubled the Yankees), won the extraordinary total of 111 games.

For a time, Casey refused to believe he could lose. The Yankees stayed on the Indians' heels and, putting together several long winning streaks, provided their manager with some cause for optimism. In a rash moment he uttered the words which have provided an epitaph for countless unwary baseball managers and football coaches: "If I lose this one, they should fire me."

Fortunately, Weiss, Topping, and Webb chose to ignore the words of the master on this subject.

Casey, in the past so sensitive to the handwriting on the wall, clung doggedly to the legend of Yankee invincibility. Only toward the end would he admit that his 1954 colossus was rooted in shifting sand. As it began to drop back of the leaders, a writer asked him what the difference was between his team and the Indians.

"Pitchers and home runs," he said ruefully. "They got too many and we ain't got enough."

He was frustrated, almost frantic, in defeat. Success had grown sweeter to him with every triumph; like a man who has climbed from poverty to great wealth, he grew panicky at the prospect of having it snatched away from him. Only the faintest hope was left him as the Yankees invaded Cleveland for a doubleheader on September 12. Before a roaring, vengeful crowd of 86,563, the biggest in baseball history, the Indians snuffed out that hope by beating the Yankees in both games. Stomping off the field, the Yankee players pushed aside the photographers who tried to take their pictures. As the writers crowded up to the clubhouse door, Stengel shouted to a special policeman, "Don't let anybody in! I don't want anybody here!"

The next day, Hal Lebovitz wrote in the Cleveland *News:* "You'll have to excuse the Yankees. After winning five straight pennants they have forgotten how to lose. Forgotten how to lose gracefully, we mean."

144

By season's end, Casey had regained his sense of humor.

Watching the Giants bowl over the Indians in four straight games contributed to Stengel's newly recaptured sense of well-being. "I think the Indians were a one-shot," he announced, before turning his steps back to Glendale for the winter. "Look at those pitchers. They're liable to go like mine did. They're not Little Neds out of the Third Reader, you know." Air of other summers had revived him.

As the 1955 training season opened, Casey's "instructual school" was emptying a bushel of new talent into his lap. Weiss' trades had added more new faces, and the Yankees were once again a formidable crew as they assembled at St. Petersburg in the spring. Casey set about molding his team with a grimness he hadn't shown since that uncertain spring of 1949. There was a stronger emphasis on fundamentals, for the Yankees of the year before had been curiously negligent in executing the routine plays that so often mean the difference in a close game. Stengel was breathing fire that spring, and his players were not the only ones to feel his wrath.

The baseball world was startled on the morning of March 27 to read that Stengel had been hauled into court the night before by Sandy Sanders, a photographer for the St. Petersburg *Independent*. Covering an exhibition game between the Yankees and the Dodgers, the photographer had planted himself in front of the dugout to take his pictures, obstructing the Yankees' view and bringing down on himself a volley of salty Stengelese. Later Sanders entered the Yankee dugout but was ordered by Stengel to leave. The order, complained Sanders, was accompanied by cuss words and a lusty kick. Casey posted bond, but the next day Sanders dropped his complaint and the matter was forgotten amidst apologies, and murmurings of "misunderstanding."

Casey had only a brief comment for the press. "I guess I forgot to say 'please.' "

Stengel was at his best as a master juggler in 1955. Injuries and an erratic pitching staff kept the Yankees in trouble most of the year. He changed his lineup constantly. Not even his healthy players knew from one day to the next where they would play or in what position they would bat. Before each game, Stengel could count only on Mantle and Berra. One would bat third, the other, fifth, according to Casey's whim, prescience, or Ouija board. He battled the Indians and White Sox down the stretch, and often had his hands full with the Tigers and Red Sox, too. Early in August he announced that the team which could put together a winning streak of eight toward the close of the season would win the pennant. As the season came into its final days the Yankees won eight straight games and walked off with the pennant. His rivals would have been justified in believing the manager of the Yankees was in league with the Evil One himself.

If such was the case, then their compact terminated at the end of the season. Mantle entered the World Series against the Dodgers with an injured leg and was badly hobbled. Casey held him out of the first two games, which the Yankees won, but then put him back in the lineup when the Series shifted to Ebbets Field. Obviously in pain, Mickey followed orders, but was a liability in the field. As the Dodgers fought back, Casey kept Mantle in action, and certain writers were critical of this stubbornness which could have jeopardized the career of his star. Casey, of course, felt justified. He wanted badly to win and thought he could only win with his best. When Mantle's helplessness became obvious, the manager took him out of the lineup.

Neither Casey's scheming nor his will to win could help the Yankees. Brooklyn, receiving strong pitching from Clem Labine and Johnny Podres, and an inspiring performance from the aging Jackie Robinson, won the Series, four games to three. Casey accepted defeat graciously. "That Podres and Labine were too much for us."

For Stengel and the Yankees the season did not end with the seventh game of the World Series. The team left shortly after for a six-week exhibition tour to Japan, a land which bows not even to Milwaukee in its devotion to America's national pastime. Most clubs would have looked upon the trip principally as a vacation. Perhaps some of the players looked on it as such in advance, but any such ideas were quickly erased by the manager. Casey does not like to lose—even when a game doesn't count. "The name Yankees stands for something all over the world," he told his players. "You fellas play every game over here as if your job depended on it. It might."

The Yankees proceeded to beat the ears off their

hosts. Meanwhile, Casey looked around him and apparently liked what he saw. He praised the Japanese players and announced to the press that the Yankees were going to hire a certain Japanese gentleman as a scout. "He's a very high class man and he can talk better than I can and his judgment will be better to judge Japanese ballplayers."

Casey also announced that, instead of flying directly back to the United States, he would escort his wife, Edna, the rest of the way around the world, "Just to prove to myself that Columbus was right."

He was next heard from in England, the scene of an early Stengel triumph. When asked if he thought that country had changed since his last visit there, he had a ready answer. "Nothing's changed. They was just as calm about me coming here this time as they was in 1924."

No one could seriously slow the Yankees' march to the pennant in 1956. Spring training that year was relatively uneventful, marked only by Don Larsen's first brush with fame. The huge pitcher had come to the Yankees from Baltimore during the winter of 1954-55, distinguished only by a reputation as a playboy and an atrocious 1954 record of three victories and twenty-one defeats. One March morning he rammed his car into a telephone pole in St. Petersburg just before dawn broke on the city. Fans and writers expected that Don's past sins would be held against him and that Stengel's justice would be swift and sure. Casey chose to ignore the shattered training

148

rules. His only comment was: "The man was either out too late or up too early."

The pennant race was marked chiefly by Mantle's brilliant season and a mammoth birthday celebration for Stengel in Kansas City. His home town had suddenly been presented with a major league franchise when the Athletics raced out of Philadelphia a step ahead of the bill collectors at the end of the 1954 season. As a Yankee visit to Kansas City almost coincided with Stengel's sixty-sixth birthday in 1956, the Athletics planned to honor the home town hero and, possibly, lure a few old chums to the ticket windows. Most such events in baseball are marred by the commercialism which lurks in the background, but Stengel and everyone connected with this party found it genuinely touching. A banquet was held in his honor, and Harry Truman led a large group of distinguished Missourians in paying homage to one of their own.

Since the Yankees played their last game at Kansas City on July 29, their manager's birthday was celebrated at Municipal Stadium a day ahead of the event. 30,000 fans warmly applauded the stooped, gray-haired veteran as he approached home plate to receive his honors before the game. He munched on a whopping portion of a huge birthday cake and astounded his old friends by weeping during a stirring testimonial. When Governor Victor Anderson of Nebraska presented him with a scroll designating him an admiral in the "Nebraska Navy," Casey worked his arms furiously in the motion of a man rowing a boat and the crowd cheered him to the rafters.

149

Then, when the game started and Casey walked out to the mound to talk to his pitcher, the partisan fans could no longer contain themselves. They booed him.

It was a great year for Casey. The Yankees romped home nine games in front and he led a healthy team into the World Series against the powerful Dodgers. The Yankees were soundly beaten in the first two games, but Casey held them together and they came back to even the Series at two games apiece. For the fifth game Casey selected Don Larsen as his pitcher, the young man who had violated the stillness of that early St. Petersburg morning with his runaway automobile. Larsen pitched the first perfect game in Series history, retiring each of the twenty-seven Dodgers he faced. In this one moment, at least, Larsen had justified Stengel's patience with him, though his baseball reputation is still precariously balanced on that one remarkable accomplishment.

The fifth game really decided the Series. Jackie Robinson's eleventh inning hit staved off the Dodgers' defeat for one day, but the Yankees overwhelmed them, 9-0, in the seventh game and the world championship returned to the Stadium, where Stengel believes it rightfully belongs.

Perhaps Casey's true value to the Yankees is revealed in moments such as this: Milton Richman recalls that the Yankee players and officials had assembled with their wives in the Waldorf-Astoria for a victory party after the final game. As time went on and Casey did not appear, someone decided to call his hotel room. Casey answered the telephone.

"Didn't even know there was a party," he said. "I

was just sitting up here figuring out a few moves that might help us next year."

And then it was 1957. There was little reason to suspect in the spring that the season would hold more than routine interest for the followers of the Yankees. Stengel's team obviously outclassed the rest of the American League by a wide margin, and whatever speculation existed was upon the identity of the National League team that would provide their opposition in the World Series. The Yankees did win the League pennant with comparative ease, but there were some uncomfortable moments for the old man along the way.

Perhaps Stengel might have had an inkling of the unusual events to come when his brilliant coaching staff was broken up for the first time. Bill Dickey became ill in Florida and returned home for the rest of the season. It was too late to hire an established coach. Stengel and Weiss then thought of Charley Keller, the home-run-hitting Yankee outfielder who, before his retirement, had been liked and admired at the Stadium. He was obviously the ideal man for the job and so Weiss summoned him from his Maryland farm. This brawny Cincinnatus abandoned his plow for the duration of the emergency, added another touch of "Old Yankee" spirit to the Stadium in 1957 and, the season over, returned home to his chores.

Joe E. Lewis has said that Copacabana is a Spanish word meaning "bring money!" For Stengel it spelled trouble. The "Copa" is one of the few brassy, flashy nightclubs in New York to survive the taxes, television and other appurtenances of the welfare state. It was only natural then that a group of the players should select this festive hall in which to celebrate Billy Martin's twenty-ninth birthday on May 16. In addition to this birthday boy, who seemed born to trouble, the party included Berra, Ford, Mantle, Hank Bauer and Johnny Kucks. Those players who were married were accompanied by their wives. During the course of the evening some words, not necessarily "Happy Birthday," were exchanged with the members of a Bronx bowling club seated at a nearby table. One of the bowlers later claimed he was slugged by Bauer, and had that heavily muscled gentleman hauled into court. The charges against Bauer were eventually dismissed, but the Yankee office did not forget that these players had, allegedly, failed to disport themselves with circumspection in a public house.

Martin, branded a troublemaker even before he came to the Yankees, was looked on by Weiss as an unwholesome influence on the younger players. Mantle, Martin's roommate, was deemed particularly susceptible to the lures of "Billy the Kid." Weiss, ignoring Martin's protestations that he was only the scapegoat in a series of unpleasant incidents, decided that the time had come to banish him to one of the increasing number of Siberias in the American League. The place of exile decided upon for Billy was Kansas City and, just before the June 15th trading deadline, he was summarily bundled off to the Athletics.

The trade was apparently made over the objections of Stengel. Casey was undoubtedly fond of his cocky second baseman. "That fresh little punk," he once said of him. "How I love him!" Yet Stengel would never allow personal relationships to interfere with the grand design of Yankee supremacy. He disagreed with Weiss, however, on the makeup of the deal itself, believing that the Yankees could have received more from the Athletics than they were willing to give up. By then, however, he had lost his power to keep Martin. The Copacabana incident had been the final blow. Calling Martin into his office after the trade had been made, he said, "Well, you're gone. You were the smartest little player I ever had. You did everything I ever asked."

Almost equally annoying to Casey were the fines imposed by Weiss on the offending revelers. It cost each of them, with the exception of Kucks, $1,000; Johnny escaped with the loss of $500, a sum more in keeping with his salary. When a reporter asked Casey whether there was trouble between Weiss and him, he shrugged and looked away. "No trouble," he said. "Weiss hasn't lost a game all season."

Only the White Sox seriously challenged the Yankees' march to their eighth pennant in nine years under Stengel. Chicago took an early lead in the race, but the Yankees soon overhauled them and began to move off by themselves. The White Sox' feeble hopes rested on a three-game series with the Yanks at Chicago late in August. Noisy and pugnaciously anti-Yankee crowds surged to Comiskey Park to try to root their heroes in, but the defending champions won all three games. As Stengel returned to the dugout after talking to his pitcher in one of the games, a fan

153

leaned out of the stands and dashed a paper cup of beer in his face.

"It was a *full* cupful, too," Casey said later. "The fella wasn't cheap about it."

When he got back to New York, Aaron Lanier, the Yankees' comptroller, told Stengel that he had seen the incident on television. "It made a marvelous picture," Lanier said.

"Did they mention the name of the beer?" Casey asked him.

"No," Lanier said.

"That's funny," Casey said. "That's the first time I ever heard of a beer on television that didn't get a plug."

That liquid blast was the last fired by Chicago. The White Sox had been subdued and the Yankees moved regally toward the 1957 World Series.

11.

If we interrupt Stengel's victorious march (a trick his American League rivals have longed to turn) to look at some of his many sides, we see more clearly why he is the most complex figure in the modern sports world. His relations with players, umpires, fans and employers, his clowning, his strategy and his outside interests all add distinct chapters to his story. He is more than just clown and tactician.

Strategy is a spectacular but not the most vital arm of the science of managing. Today especially, when all players are painfully aware of their individual rights, a manager must know his men thoroughly and handle them in such a way that he will get the most out of each of them. Because he urgently hopes to be remembered as the greatest manager baseball has known, Casey's ties with the men under him play a major role in any account of his success. These relationships are often as intricately spun as his own way of speaking.

As we have seen, Stengel's efforts to handle his players at Brooklyn and Boston broke down because of their incompetence. He eventually came to regard this refractory material with amused detachment, even open sarcasm. When he took over the Yankees the shoe was on the other foot. That superb collection of players, basking in past glory, was inclined to look at Casey as a broken-down clown who had stumbled by chance into the throne room. His shrewdness and his unique knowledge of the game quickly changed the Yankees' opinion of him. However, at first he moved cautiously in their presence, and treated Di-Maggio, in particular, with appropriate respect.

In 1949 he gave full rein to his ailing older players, DiMaggio, Keller, Henrich and Rizzuto, as they worked themselves into shape. He refused to push them, even under the prodding of the writers, who felt he was indecisive. While DiMaggio sat out the first sixty-five games of that season, Casey held his peace and let Joe come to him with the word that he was finally ready to play. Contrast this with his handling of Mantle in recent years when he often pushed that crippled and reluctant young man into the lineup for important games.

The difference is, of course, that these are "his" players. They came to Casey as rookies or nonentities; he watched them grow and he had a hand in their development. Some of them have disliked him. Page, the relief pitcher whom he brought back to stardom in 1949, believed that Stengel ruined him through overwork. Not long ago he said of Casey in bitter tones, "He was a clown in Boston, and he's still a clown."

Woodling, whom Casey had humiliated with his pantomime on the dugout steps during the 1950 World Series, never forgave him. Many of the other players, believing they should play regularly, have resented the eternal shuffling which has kept them idle so often. Gordon Cobbledick of the Cleveland

156

Plain Dealer recalls a pennant-clinching party tossed by the Yankees in 1952. Stengel was entertaining a cluster of writers in one corner of the room when his husky outfielder, Hank Bauer, squeezed past him on his way to the door. The writers noticed that Bauer did not offer his manager a word of congratulations, or even a smile, as he went past. Casey looked after him and grinned. "Look at him," he said with obvious relish. "The big lug hates my guts."

Sometimes a reporter will ask a Yankee player why Stengel ordered a certain piece of strategy and he will get the off-the-record reply, "How do I know why he did it? He's crazy!"

Yet they seem to have the utmost faith in him. His policy has been that of the former Yale football coach, Herman Hickman, who kept his men "sullen but not mutinous." During a television interview while the Yankees were behind in a World Series several years ago, Mantle was asked what he thought of his team's chances. "We'll be okay," Mickey answered casually. "Ol' Case will think of something."

Even Woodling in his last years with the Yankees grudgingly admitted that the constant juggling of the lineup which was a source of acute irritation for the players had eventually helped each of them. "I don't like to be taken out when a lefty's pitching against us," Woodling said, "but I'll be darned if the player Stengel puts in there doesn't always do a bangup job and wind up winning us a lot of ball games. Those games add up to pennants for us and, of course, more money. I guess you can't fault the old man for that."

Like any successful leader, Stengel shows his loyalty

for the men who have served him well. When Irv Noren's injured knees had slowed him down to such an extent that Weiss wanted to trade him, Casey flew to his outfielder's defense. "How do you think he banged up them knees? He banged them up running into fences for the Yankees."

Casey has always admired physical courage and aggressiveness. Enos Slaughter, the balding, hustling veteran, is one of his favorites. Sitting in the dugout one day while talking to the reporters, Stengel pointed to Slaughter, who was in the batting cage. "A good man. He broke a shoulder for me once, trying to make a catch. You can still see the scar where they operated on him." He drew an imaginary line across his chest with a brisk stroke of his hand. "He will slide for you and dive for a low hit ball and hit the ground and he will hit the wall for you if he has to." Stengel sat back and rubbed his chin. "Slaughter was brought up right."

He always has the welfare of his players in mind. If one of them has been asked to appear on a television show, Casey badgers him to demand a healthy fee in exchange for his time. "Don't help those people with their shows for coffee-and-cake money. You're a Yankee—the best. Get some money from them." In spring training he has posted on the clubhouse bulletin board a list of the tips the players should leave for waiters, bellhops and chamber maids (though cynics familiar with the inveterate stinginess of ballplayers have suggested that Stengel supplied this information for the welfare of the hotel's hired help, not the Yankees). Another example was the day President Eisenhower attended the opening game of the 1956 World Series at Ebbets Field. In pre-game ceremonies, Ike shook hands with Stengel, Dodger manager Walt Alston and each of the Brooklyn players. Ike then turned and started for his seat behind the Dodger dugout. Casey matter-of-factly tugged at the President's sleeve and motioned with his head toward *his* players. Each of the Yankees received a warm presidential handshake.

When one of Casey's players lets him down, even though he is a star, he will hear about it. Casey bows to no one in his admiration for Whitey Ford, the cocky southpaw, but he will occasionally remind Whitey that he still holds the whip. In 1954 Ford arrived for spring training twenty pounds overweight. The season passed its first month and Ford still had not shown Casey that he was working himself into shape. He had been hit hard in several pitching assignments. Late in May Casey put him into a game with the Red Sox and, though Whitey obviously had nothing on the ball, let him stay in to take an unmerciful pounding. Whitey got the idea this time, and applied himself with more diligence to his conditioning.

Stengel seldom refers to his players by name. This is a distinction he denies all but his stars, the top columnists, and a select few among "his" writers. In discussing his team, he will refer to "the third baseman's" arm, or the speed of "my leftfielder," and only those listeners familiar with the makeup of the team will be able to follow him accurately. So high has Berra risen in his estimation that Casey often refers to him slyly as "Mr. Berra."

Perhaps Casey, on first seeing Yogi, felt a close bond with him because everybody said that the young catcher did not look like a ballplayer. They had said the same thing of the bow-legged, long-armed Stengel almost forty years before. Yogi could butcher a play as well as any of the clowns who had played for Casey at Brooklyn or Boston, but Casey saw that his reflexes were those of an athlete, and his batting eye was almost as sharp as Paul Waner's had been. Here was at least the raw material of a fine ballplayer. When he announced his coaching staff for the 1949 season, a significant exchange took place between him and the press. "I'm signing Jim Turner to coach my pitchers and Frank Crosetti to coach my infielders and Bill Dickey to coach my catchers."

"Your catchers?" a reporter asked. "You mean Yogi?"

"Well, yes," Casey said. "I guess you could say that."

Dickey worked on Yogi's catching and Stengel nagged him about swinging at bad pitches, and soon a great player began to emerge. Dickey performed his task well, for Yogi became a smooth and alert receiver; neither Casey nor anyone else has ever been able to restrain him from going for bad pitches while at bat, but the eager Yogi seems to hit squarely anything he can reach. Stengel's greatest contribution to his success was probably encouragement. He wisely saw that Berra, in those early days, doubted himself

160

and was easily discouraged. The manager never let pass an opportunity for boosting his ego. He drummed into him the thought that he was already the best catcher in baseball. If Yogi walked by him in a hotel lobby or a dining car, Casey would nimbly switch the subject to Berra and raise his voice. "There goes the greatest—that kid. Nobody can touch him. The greatest!"

Yogi, of course, was flattered by all of this and began to believe at least some of it. His latent ability appeared with his added confidence. He went right on hitting bad pitches and winning games, and Stengel relished every bit of it. "I remember we had a home run hitting contest before a game one night and Yogi is going up there. Every hitter is going to have five swings and I say to somebody, 'He won't be up there long.' They pitch five balls to him and he didn't let any go by, no matter where they are. He swings at them and hits three in the stands and he is back in no time and he wins the contest."

Where Stengel's relationship with Yogi has almost always been benign, that with Martin was stormy. He had first managed Martin at Oakland. Billy then was a fresh, unpolished kid right off the streets, and Casey didn't awe him any more than the cops or the neighborhood bullies had. When the manager tried to show him the right way to pivot on the doubleplay, Martin bristled. "I don't see what's wrong with my way," he snapped. "I got quick hands. I got quick feet."

"You ain't on the dance floor jitterbugging," Casey said sharply.

161

But Martin came right back at him. "Don't knock my way just because you can't do it."

Telling the story later, Casey remarked, "Another kid I would make take off his uniform and go home, but not him because he wants to play so bad it sticks out all over him."

On one occasion Casey countered an insolent remark with, "You talk big, kid."

Martin scowled at him. "I play big, too."

Five years later, with the Yankees, Casey and his pet were still battling.

Billy was as high-spirited off the field as he was on it, and Yankee officials, notably Weiss, later questioned the wisdom of making him the roommate of the impressionable Mantle. They ate together, they went to movies together, and they went out on the town together. Yet there was nothing really bad in either of them. Both were a couple of kids—one from the slums of Oakland, California, the other from a small Oklahoma town—who had fame thrust upon them and who had never completely escaped their adolescence. One of their favorite pastimes, in the privacy of their hotel room, was to walk slowly toward each other, whip out imaginary six-shooters and begin blasting away, shouting "bang-bang," just as they had seen it done in the Westerns. Then they would fall to arguing over who was the fastest on the draw.

One afternoon at the Stadium, Stengel watched the two of them play a lively game of catch in front of the dugout. "You know what they're doing?" he asked a reporter. "They're trying to see who can break the other one's finger first. They want to see who is tougher."

Of all Casey's relationships with his players, that with Mantle is probably the strangest. Stengel, childless, has put his devotion and his hopes into his players. He speaks with the bitterness of a wronged father when a favorite lets him down, as in the "Copa" incident. His feelings toward Mantle, a shy, partly withdrawn boy, obviously differ from the affection in which he holds Berra and Martin. As columnist Milton Gross has pointed out, Stengel saw in this wonder boy the promise of a monument which he could leave behind him when he retired from baseball. DiMaggio, Henrich, Rizzuto, Mize and, to some extent, even Berra, he had inherited. Others, such as Martin, groomed by him, were valuable players, but none had the potential of this broad-backed Oklahoma boy. Casey believed that, with any luck, he could transform Mantle into the greatest player of all time.

Casey hasn't had the luck he hoped for. Mantle's legs are notoriously fragile and he has been useless to the Yankee manager at times when he needed him most. Mickey was hobbled badly during the 1955 and 1957 World Series, the only two Stengel has lost. Even more vexing has been Mantle's failure to make the most of his ability. To squander the greatest natural talent in baseball is a sin for which Casey will never completely forgive him; he remembers how he himself had to hustle and scheme and practice to make good in the big leagues. "You tell him something," Casey once said, "and he acts like you tell him nothing."

Did he tell Mantle to rest an injured leg, that young man would inevitably aggravate it romping on a basketball court. Did he tell him not to risk straining his arm by throwing knuckle balls or other trick pitches before a game, Mickey would look carefully around him to make sure that the manager was not in sight and then go back to throwing his trick pitches. Did he tell him to stop trying to "kill" the ball, Mickey would swing all the harder. The perpetual war he has waged against Mantle's obstinacy has been the source of most of Casey's unhappy moments with the Yankees.

He has used all his arts of reasoning and cajoling, rather than sarcasm or sabre-rattling, to awaken Mickey to his own limitless possibilities. After striking out one day, Mantle stormed back into the dugout and petulantly kicked the water cooler. Casey looked at him sadly. "That water cooler ain't striking you out, son."

He has tried to point out to him the things which the more alert DiMaggio discovered for himself. "I had to teach him to run after fly balls in the outfield looking back over his shoulder which DiMag was so great at, and not run looking down at the ground. 'They don't have plowed fields up here, son,' I tell him, 'and you don't have to watch out for furrows or trenches at the same time because this is the big league and the fields is all level and they have groundskeepers and everything.'"

It would not be true to say that Mantle has been a

164

failure, or that another generation will not look back on him as one of the greatest sluggers of all time. It is just that Stengel set such lofty standards for him that he is disappointed when his protégé does not apply himself to his career as Casey believes he should. It is inconceivable to the old man that anyone could leave a single stone unturned in the pursuit of greatness. This endless struggle for perfection has been a part of Casey's life since those early days in Maysville, and it has driven him to find new and better methods of winning at an age when most men of his wealth would have returned home to rock on the porch and count their money. Like Caesar, Stengel strenuously maintains that nothing has been accomplished while even the smallest detail remains unfinished. It is a philosophy which builds empires and bedevils self-satisfied ballplayers.

12.

NEITHER AGE, wealth nor position has changed Casey Stengel. They have not added reserve or austerity to his bearing and, contrary to popular belief, they have not materially enlarged his brain. Despite years of living in big cities, he is basically the same clown who came out of Kansas City almost fifty years ago. Despite his triumphs with the Yankees, he is the same manager who limped home with his outclassed forces in Brooklyn and Boston. His success, like that of any leader, can be traced ultimately to the skill with which he handles his men. He is known to the public, however, as a great showman, constantly on stage, whether mimicking one of his bosses, recalling his early days, or outmaneuvering his rivals. He is unique both as clown and tactician.

He is a clown in the best sense, his humor being based on a complete awareness of what is going on around him and a talent for mimicry that is seldom equaled even by professionals. While his wit is quick, it is often sarcastic and sometimes crude, a relic of his early rough-and-tumble days. When asked one day about a certain pitcher, he said, "He's very skinny. In fact he don't even have a muscle in his arm. He just holds the ball out and lets his pulse carry it up to the plate."

166

Another time, he took one of his pitchers aside and asked him, "Why do you keep throwing your curve ball when you get in a jam? I keep telling you it's lousy. If you ever got a chance to hit against it, you'd *never* throw it."

He does not disdain the use of biting wit if by it he can embarrass an umpire. Some years ago he disagreed with a call made by Charley Moran. When he saw that further strong language might goad the irritated umpire into tossing him out of the game, Casey's face softened and he good-naturedly asked Moran, "Say, didn't you used to coach the Praying Colonels?"

"Yes," Moran said, softening a bit, too.

Casey's face hardened again. "Well, I was just wondering what they was praying for. A new coach?"

Casey is not a practical joker but, like all of us, he cannot pass up a golden opportunity. Talking to a group of writers on the field at St. Petersburg one spring, he saw John Drebinger of the New York *Times* approaching him. John wears a hearing aid. Casey quickly tipped off his listeners that he had mischief in mind. Drebinger came up to the group and, suitably wired for sound, cocked an attentive ear to catch whatever news the manager had for the press. To his consternation, John saw Stengel's lips moving and the writers frantically scribbling in their notebooks, but he could not hear a sound. He hastily adjusted his hearing aid, and listened again. Casey's lips still moved, he gestured dramatically, and the writers continued to take down the news. Drebinger turned his gadget on as high as it would go. Still there was no sound.

167

Afraid now that he was missing an important announcement, he leaned toward Stengel and said, "Sorry, Casey, but I seem to be working on a dead battery."

The manager put his lips to John's ear and shouted, "Is this better?"

It is said that sound waves ricocheted inside Drebinger's skull for the rest of the afternoon.

Occasionally Stengel resorts to fiction to enliven a monologue about his early days. He once entertained an audience with this apocryphal tale: "When I was playing for the Giants, the fans got on me and they gave me a pretty fair booing. I decided to get back at them. I came out of the dugout swinging as many bats as a fella can carry without a mule. The crowd started booing right away, so when I got to the plate I gave them the Babe Ruth routine—pointing to the bleachers like that's where I'm going to hit the ball. That shut them up for a second."

Here Casey paused so that his listeners might savor the audacity of his gesture. "Then I took three fast strikes and ran for the dugout."

In certain medieval manuscripts the artist has distracted the readers from the text by painting little grotesques and arabesques around the edges of his page; the text is drab in contrast to the art. Stengel's own grotesque and arabesque gestures are fascinating in themselves, yet they cannot draw one's attention from his speech, which, too, is incredibly involved. The writer who attempts to catch the essence of Casey's monologues is usually doomed to failure. Many have tried to approximate his way of speaking by liberally sprinkling their version of it with "which," and by tossing in *non sequiturs* at appropriate places. The result often is as far from authentic "Stengelese" as an old daguerreotype was from the sunset it pretended to depict. "The human ear is a wonderful instrument," Red Smith once wrote, "but not so wonderful as the Stengel larynx."

Red Smith, like others despairing of capturing the "real" Casey in print, resorted to science in his quest and caught him in the following manner, in the New York *Herald Tribune* on May 6, 1953:

"Students of Stengelese, which is a live language only superficially resembling Sanscrit, have endeavored for years to capture in print the special quality, the pure body and flavor, the rich, crunchy goodness of Mr. Casey Stengel's speech.

"They have not succeeded. The human ear is a wonderful instrument, but not so wonderful as the Stengel larynx. The mother tongue of the Yankees' manager is an oil that rolls over the consciousness but is not retained. The pencil of a stenographer may catch a phrase and hold it, quivering in beauty like a butterfly on an entomologist's pin, but something escapes in translation from notebook to type.

"A recording is required for proper reproduction, and lately a record has been obtained. It is not new; it was cut last summer at a reunion of old Yankee stars which Mr. Stengel graced with a formal address.

"The transcription is offered in reverence. In his introduction the toastmaster has remarked that he guesses Casey wouldn't mind having some of the former Yankees back on the team. What follows is pure

Stengel, preserved in wax as at Mme Tussaud's or like rare viands in aspic:

" 'Well, that's the greatest remark that you ever made. After bein' a manager that had had major league clubs in the National League and in the American League and in minor leagues I would have to say to come back and run the Yankees I was, uh, very thrilled with some of the men that I saw today.

" 'I don't wanta go back inta the years at the present time, but I'll start in with the last three years since I been a manager.

" 'We had Mr. DiMaggio that walked out there today and when I tell you that DiMaggio with the cheers he received every one of 'em shoulda been given by myself and I shoulda yelled all winter during my off season because of the success that the club had with him at the bat and the wonderful ketches that he made in the outfield.

" 'I also had Tommy Handricks who was one of the greatest hitters that I ever saw in my life to walk up and git the ball that he wanted in a pinch and I also had Mr. Keller who was one of the greatest outfielders I ever saw in my life as far as puttin' effort inta his work—strong, just wouldn't give in and he always believed and all three of those men, that a manager run a ball club which is an amazing thing.

" 'They thought that all you had to do at the Yankees is to be there on time, tend to your own business off the field and when they said play ball be sure you go out and play hard and play clean.

" 'The only thing I can say for the Yankees today is this: that it's a young club that was reee-built and in-

170

steada dropping to fifth or sixth place with the number of people that we have in our organization that're now playing ball and the number of men that've gone to the service it's that carry-on spirit that the Yankees have and everybody in this country wants somebody to be a Yankee or live like a Yankee which don't mean just baseball but to be somebody for the United States.

" 'So disregard any, uh, wonderful, uh, lauding or anything of my ability you'll have to say that I been carried along with the wonderful thing that makes the Yankees carry on and I don't blame people for bein' jealous of it we love it we want everybody to try and beat us but don't get mad at us because we're a splendid outfit and we try hard to win and respect everybody that beats us.' "

During the 1957 World Series, the *Ladies' Home Journal* placed an advertisement in *The New Yorker;* it was a testimonial to the *Journal,* "the world's greatest authority on women," from Stengel, "the world's greatest authority." The testimonial, written in an ad man's version of Stengelese, was accompanied by translations at suitable points. It read, in part:

"It's like they (*Ladies' Home Journal*) keep saying, men and women are different. Because why? Well, take ballplayers. They (women) won't ever make as good a hitter as some of my fellas. Maybe, but not many of them. All you hafta do is look. . . . Which of the two are best—men or women? Let's say it's lucky for you there is two."

Buzzie Bavasi, a vice-president of the Dodgers, tells of an evening spent in the enthralling occupation of listening to pure Stengelese:

171

"A couple of us had dinner at Al Schacht's restaurant and Casey came over to join us afterwards," Bavasi says. "That was about eight o'clock. Well, he started to talk as soon as he sat down and he didn't stop until about one o'clock and I think I was laughing every minute of that time. Casey was telling stories or parts of stories and slipping in comments on this and that and I never heard anything as funny in my life. When I finally got out of there and was on my way home I tried to think back to what was so funny. I couldn't remember a sentence he said or single out a story he told. It was just the way he talked and his gestures and the faces he made."

When Casey is telling a story, his audience does not have to follow his words. It knows by his gestures and expressions what, and even whom, he is talking about. One awed listener reported after spending an evening with him: "When Casey was talking about a catcher who looked like a horse, he not only looked more like a horse than the catcher did, he looked more like a horse than Man O' War."

Like every performer, Casey has his "classic." Those who have seen it insist that his most spectacular routine (aside from passing his kidney stone, perhaps) is his description of two Boston outfielders, Johnny Cooney and Max West. Demonstrating Cooney, a graceful outfielder, he will move around under phantom fly balls, finally emphasizing his point by drifting gracefully back to pluck an imaginary ball off an imaginary wall. Suddenly he becomes West, a clumsy outfielder. "Now I had another boy who wasn't so graceful," he explains. Here he wobbles back un-

172

der a fly ball, turns, puts his head down and runs full tilt into the very real wall of the room in which he is performing. He then falls heavily to the ground, still clutching the "ball" firmly in his fist, and says, " 'My boy,' I told West, 'you have a great pair of hands.' "

At the winter meetings in Columbus one year, Casey finished a long speech, then asked his audience if there was any one story they wanted to hear before he sat down.

"Tell them the one about Cooney and West," Red Patterson of the Dodgers shouted.

Casey began to talk again, went on for another hour and a half, and forgot to mention either Cooney or West.

That memorable weekend in 1934 when his lowly Dodgers knocked Bill Terry's Giants out of the pennant race affords an example of Stengel's combined abilities as actor and tactician. Casey, suspecting that the Giants had stolen his bunt sign, told his players just before the Saturday game that the sign for the bunt was to be ignored. Late in the game Tony Cuccinello came up with two runners on base, and Casey flashed the "bunt" sign. The Giant infielders quickly moved in and Tony slashed a base hit past them.

"I made out I was very mad at Cuccinello," Stengel recalls. "It was one of the best acts of my life, because the Giants figured Tony had disobeyed me. The next day the same situation came up and I gave Tony the 'bunt' sign again. Those Giant infielders came running in again and Tony busts another base hit past them. As the ball goes by I can hear their third baseman, Travis Jackson, yell like he's crying. Those were two very big hits Tony got and they helped us win both those ball games."

Casey was criticized a few years ago for sending up a couple of his pitchers as pinch-hitters. The Yankees were being beaten by Bob Feller at the Stadium and, with the tying run on second base in the ninth inning, Stengel needed a pinch-hitter. Feller, once the fastest pitcher in the game, had lost much of his speed and now resorted to guile when he found himself in trouble. On the Yankee bench were several hard-swinging young bruisers, capable of hitting the ball out of sight, but also likely to be fooled by the veteran Cleveland pitcher. Besides, Casey didn't need a home run. All he wanted was a single to bring home the tying run from second. He selected Ed Lopat, his left-handed pitcher, because of his sharp eye at the plate and his ability to poke the ball through the infield. Lopat went up and grounded out. Casey looked around him and selected another pitcher, Tommy Byrne, for the same reasons. Byrne also grounded out and the Yankees lost the game. Casey still believes he had percentage on his side, yet he is quick to admit his fallibility.

One night Luke Easter beat the Yankees with a three-run home run in the bottom of the ninth at Cleveland. When the team returned to the Stadium, John Drebinger asked Casey about the nightmarish events of that inning.

"Now I'll tell you," the manager said, leaning toward Drebinger. "I blew that one myself. You see, they had two men on and three tough hitters coming up. I brought in my relief pitcher, Ferrick, who is a righthander. He got the first hitter out and so I went out to the mound to talk to him about Easter. I had a lefty warming up and I was going to bring him in to pitch to Easter, who hits left. But Ferrick says he can get this fella, too, so I says 'Okay, but don't give him anything low to hit. Keep it high.'

"I just get back into the dugout when I remember that the only reason I got this pitcher in there is because he has a very good low ball which he gets many hitters out with. I don't even know if he can throw a high ball. Then I hear a terrific roar from the crowd and I see the ball going out of the park. I hit my head on the roof of the dugout and everything goes black. I hope that clout will straighten out my thinking."

Casey has no illusions about his indispensability. If one of his players gets into an argument with an umpire, Stengel will invariably race to the scene and draw the umpire's attention to himself with some heated words of his own. He firmly believes that, if anyone is going to be thumbed from the game, it is far better for the team to lose its manager than a key player. Perhaps he also believes that he is providing the umpire with a more articulate opponent.

Stengel is also willing to stand corrected. Once, after making out a lineup, he gave it to the batboy to post in the dugout. Idly checking the lineup, the boy noticed that Casey had listed two rightfielders for the game. When he brought the mistake to the manager's attention, Casey gave him twenty-five dollars.

Such lapses on his part are extremely rare. As someone has said, he makes out his batting order like a woman choosing a hat. Each day it is the object of infinite care. During certain seasons Stengel has fielded over a hundred different lineups. One day Casey presented his lineup card to the umpires at home plate, and they in turn handed it to Jimmy Dykes, the opposing manager. Dykes glanced at it and handed it back to Stengel. "You made a mistake here, Casey," Dykes said.

Startled, Casey carefully inspected it. "I don't see any mistakes. Where?"

"I just figured there must be a mistake somewhere," Dykes said. "It's the same lineup you used yesterday."

The logic behind Stengel's scrambled lineups may be inscrutable, but there is little doubt that they are effective. A man who batted fifth and clouted four hits one day may be dropped to eighth in the batting order the next day. It is almost always an adventure for Yankee players to inspect the lineup card that Casey posts in the dugout before each game. Here they find out if they are going to play, what position, and where they will bat. In 1957 Casey seemed extremely fond of moving rookie Tony Kubek around. Tony played shortstop, third base, and all outfield positions. During the World Series a Milwaukee writer, especially interested in Kubek because he is a native of that city, asked Stengel where Tony would be stationed for the opening game at County Stadium.

Casey looked out across the field as if he were lost in thought. Then he said, "Well, I'll tell you. I understand his family is going to be at the game and I'm going to find out where they've got seats and then play the boy there."

176

Stengel found in Brooklyn and Boston that a manager can think for twenty-four hours a day and nothing will come of it unless he can get his players to think while they are on the field. "You gotta remember one thing," he once told a team. "In this game you're on your own. There's twenty-five guys on every other club talking about you—what you hit, what you don't hit, how you pitch, and so on. Unless you work and practice and ask questions and not let well enough alone you'll be out of a job."

It has been a large part of Casey's success in New York that he has been provided with players who can and will follow this advice. The Yankees have a professional attitude. Many of them don't like being "platooned," but Casey tells them, "Do it my way and I'll get you more money." They understand that, and they like it, too.

Casey a clown? Leo Durocher, a combative egotist who is not addicted to blowing other people's horns, has some strong ideas on Stengel. "He's a genius," Leo says. "It's unfair to other managers to compare them with him."

Casey, one must conclude, is like a pickpocket who tickles his victim while lifting his watch.

13.

"CASEY BABBLES on in front of an audience," one veteran writer claims, "because he just gets flustered. He's afraid to stop talking, so he spouts out anything that comes into his head."

That writer is almost alone in his opinion, yet it is an indication of the contradictions in Casey's character. The boundary between the man and the actor is as indistinct as the logic of his monologues. "If somebody talks as if he's crazy," wrote a Midwestern sports editor in a column about Stengel, "there are only two possible explanations. Either he is crazy, or he's putting on an act." When listening to Stengel discourse on the nature of things, one feels certain of being in the presence of a consummate actor.

In a story some years ago, *Time* magazine reported that Casey was the model for Ring Lardner's *Alibi Ike*. While it is true that he did supply Lardner with background for some of his stories, anyone who has been within earshot of Casey is aware that he did not sit for the portrait of a man whose conversation was confined to apologies. The wise-cracking Carey of that story is closer to the real Stengel.

There is not much big-city sophistication about Stengel. John McGraw, for whom he played and with whom he will always be compared as a manager, shook

178

off the mark of the small towns and became as much a part of New York as Jimmy Walker and Al Smith. Casey remains strangely alien to his surroundings. He has never been the popular New York idol, nor the familiar figure along Broadway, that McGraw was. He still wears on his face the map of Kansas City.

In keeping with the lofty position he now occupies, he has tried to disassociate himself from the roistering picture of the young Stengel, a picture which he long helped to perpetuate through his amusing stories. When *Time* magazine wanted to illustrate an article with a photograph of the police leading him away after his fight with Phil Weinert, he strenuously objected. When John Lardner, writing an article about Phil Douglas, a Giant teammate of Casey's, asked him to recall some of the barroom tales he used to tell of those days, Stengel declined. As far as he is concerned, they never happened. Or, if they did, they happened to somebody else.

He bitterly resented a magazine story in which the writer poked fun at his wardrobe. "He dresses like a burlesque actor," was the line that particularly hurt him. "I don't know how a burlesque actor dresses," he said, "but I do know I buy my clothes in a store in Los Angeles which is more expensive than I can afford."

Both estimates fall somewhat short of the truth. Winning ball clubs and producing oil wells have relieved Casey of the necessity for buying paper suitcases and two-pants suits of clothes. On the other hand, he is a conservative dresser, preferring suits of dark

179

blue and gray, although occasionally he will appear at the Stadium in a sports outfit. His snap-brim hats and conservative top coats are also in keeping with the Yankees' ideas of how their employees should dress. In his taste for fashions, at least, Casey is more at home in the fastidious décor of the team's Fifth Avenue offices than he is at the stage door of the Palace Theater.

There is no doubt that a large, appreciative and, perhaps most important, distinguished audience stimulates Casey to put on his best shows. Then "Ol' Case," as he affectionately refers to himself, creates a figure as close as possible to that which the newspapers and magazines have nurtured. But he is not always on stage. A reporter, arriving early at the Stadium, will occasionally find Casey alone in his office, and then the mask is often dropped. He will discuss his ball club in sober tones, shrewdly analyze the rest of the league, and talk about a prospective trade—in phrases almost devoid of accepted Stengelisms and which reveal a wider vocabulary than has usually been assigned him by his biographers. It is only then that the interviewer is allowed a glimpse of the solid foundation of Casey's success, a foundation that is almost perpetually obscured in clouds of twisted rhetoric, irrelevant anecdotes, and baseball strategy.

One of the bases of his success is his extraordinary memory. It operates whether he is in quiet conversation in his office or the heady throes of a dugout spectacular. Every item of interest to him, no matter how flimsy its relation to his world or how questionable

180

its source, is picked up and filed in the crowded archives of his mind. It might be that a National League writer, in town for a visit, happens to mention that a Cincinnati pitcher has trouble fielding a bunt. Several years may pass before the Yankees face that same pitcher, but when they do, Casey will recall this scrap of information and investigate it for himself. The writer may prove to have been wrong, or the pitcher may have improved as a fielder, but one way or another, Casey will remember it.

As another example, a man in a hotel may mention in Casey's presence that a new highway is planned for western Arizona. This will ring a bell somewhere in his mind. A year before he might have heard of a cement plant in that approximate area. He will quickly surmise that the highway contractors will buy their cement from nearby plants. The next morning his broker will be directed to buy stock in the cement company.

When they contrast this omnivorous memory to his apparent inability to retain the names of most of those around him, certain writers and players are mildly resentful. "I've been covering the Yankees for years," one writer complained, "and he never gave any sign that he knew my name until one night in spring training. Then he took us all to a friend's house for dinner, where he had to introduce me to the host. As it was, he just mumbled my last name."

Still, Casey has no difficulty in making his audience know whom he is talking about. A shrug of the shoulders, a wrinkling of the face, an inflection of the voice, all serve to identify his subject.

If he doesn't always refer to "his" writers by name, he does bestow other favors on them. He is aware of their problems and, unlike most baseball men, does his best to accommodate himself to their needs. Realizing that the needs of a man who works for an afternoon paper differ from those of the morning paper writers, he will try to work out special angles for him. He keeps in mind that a morning paper man may have to turn in a story that will fill space until the result of a night game is known. In the dugout before a game, he will have ready a list of items that each writer can use for his early story—how Mantle's sore leg is healing, why Berra's split finger may keep him out of the lineup, the identity of the next day's pitcher, all systematically ticked off on his fingers.

Immediately after the Yankees had clinched the 1952 pennant in Philadelphia, a horde of photographers rushed into their clubhouse to pose Stengel in the attitudes of ecstasy required of him under such circumstances. "Gentlemen, gentlemen," Stengel said, silencing them, like a holy man quieting troubled waters, "in your time and turn. I am talking with the writers covering my club, and with me they come first."

He is especially solicitous of young reporters with his club. Several years ago, a writer, who had been assigned briefly to the Yankees and was then transferred to another team, went over to Casey in the dugout to thank him for his graciousness.

"Don't mention it, kid," the manager said, with a wave of his hand. "You done splendid."

182

A visible glow suffused the young reporter's face as he left the Stadium.

Despite his apparent interest in other matters, baseball remains Casey's chief interest. He relates everything else to it. "He doesn't talk about anything else," his wife, Edna, has said. "He doesn't think about anything else. He just doesn't want to do anything else." He seems to have accumulated his money almost absentmindedly. Edna remains at home much of the summer, handling the various Stengel enterprises, while he travels with the team, picking up at random the scraps of information which add to his wealth and passing the greatest part of his time living and talking and dreaming baseball.

In New York Stengel lives at the Essex House, a fashionable hotel overlooking Central Park and only a few blocks from the Yankees' Fifth Avenue office. He and Edna dine with friends or baseball people at certain steak houses around midtown Manhattan (like most baseball players, Casey is an inveterate beef-eater) and occasionally appear at one of the larger gathering places such as Toots Shor's. He is justifiably annoyed by writers who inquire about his personal habits, for no matter what his schedule the previous night may have been, he is invariably the first man at the ball park in the morning.

Even when he is in bed early he does not get a full night's sleep. He brings the newspapers home with him, reads them all before turning out the light, and then settles his head on his pillow to outstare whatever baseball problem presently confronts him. In the morning he has the latest papers sent up, and goes through them for the results of games played the night before. He carefully studies the box scores of every game in both leagues. "Sometimes you have a chance to get a fella from the National League," he says, "so you gotta keep tabs on them, too."

After eating a hearty breakfast of bacon and eggs, Casey heads for the ball park. He needs the breakfast. In the swirl of events at the Stadium he may forget to eat lunch.

For Casey, winter is a time of restless hibernation. He has a lovely eleven-room home in Glendale, California, gleaming white and set amid a rose garden and an orange grove, but to him it doesn't compare with the towering stands and the green expanse of Yankee Stadium. "What's the sense of having a beautiful home like this," Edna once asked him, "if you're never here to enjoy it?"

Those were the days when she still held out hope that he would retire after winning one or two pennants for the Yankees. So, Casey relaxes as best he can in the glass-walled garden house, prowls through the orange grove and dips into his swimming pool, and all the while he is looking to spring training. On weekends he occasionally goes to Los Angeles for a football game, and there are the inevitable banquets to be attended during the winter. The banquets were occasions on which he could talk baseball, of course, but they were endless, and he found that they left him limp by the time he was ready to leave for training camp. When someone asked him how he was able to restrict his attendance at banquets, he offered one of his fabrications.

"I just stunk out the place," he said, "and so they stopped asking me back."

It is ironic that McGraw, who grew to be much more of a city slicker than Casey has, lost a great deal of money in his investments, while Casey has done very well. He stoutly denies, however, that he is an oil magnate. "The oil wells," he will tell you, "are something like an annuity. They pay a steady income, but nothing sensational."

His other investments have included a theater, an apartment house in Glendale, and a restaurant chain into which he, tennis promoter Jack Kramer, and football coach Frankie Albert have put money. He also holds stock in the Glendale National Bank, of which he was recently made a member of the board.

Although Casey is permanently settled in Glendale, he still has ties in Kansas City, where his brother, Grant, and his sister, Louise, live. Grant, whose determination is just as strong as Casey's, is very proud of his illustrious brother, but he would never accept help of any kind from him. Until his health failed several years ago he drove for the Yellow Cab Company there. Whenever Casey travels by air, he names Louise the beneficiary of his plane insurance.

Edna, who for a long time worried about Casey's health, talked him into taking her on a winter vacation trip to Puerto Rico. On their first night in San Juan they had just settled themselves in bed when they heard a muffled roar in the distance. Casey leaped

185

into action like an old fire dog at the sound of the alarm.

"That sounds like a ball game," he muttered, hastily pulling on his clothes. "I guess I'd better go have a look."

It was incidents such as this which began to convince Edna that Casey's retirement was a long way off. For a while he assured her that he was going to win "just one more," and then settle down in Glendale. "One year when we were in New York," Edna recalls, "he told me he was going to quit. On an afternoon soon after he sent me out to buy a hat, and while I was gone he walked over to the Yankee office and signed a new contract."

Edna has been the perfect mate for Casey. Tall and attractive, she is gracious in her position as the wife of the manager of the Yankees, and remarkably understanding toward her husband. She has come to accept the fact that despite his years, the gale of life still blows high through her famous husband.

"He has only one life," she says, "and that's baseball. This is the way he's happy, and so I'm happy for him."

She knows that to take Casey out of baseball would be to cut his stage from under him. Some who know him well say he will retire when he wins his eighth world championship; his victory in the 1956 World Series was his sixth, and he needs two more to break Joe McCarthy's record of seven. There are others who say that Casey will keep pushing back his retirement as it confronts him, and that he will cling to the job

186

as long as health and his general manager allow him to.

It is impossible to imagine Casey out of baseball, just as it is impossible to separate the actor in him from the rest of the man. Thomas Mann once asked, what is the real glow worm—the alluring gleam in the dark, or the ugly little creature we hold in our hands? No one has claimed that Casey is an alluring gleam, nor would anyone even suggest he resembles that other object. Yet the comic mask, like a radiant glow, is an essential part of Casey the man. It is a paradox that, when he is mimicking others, he is most himself.

14.

THE CLOSING WEEKS of the 1957 season were not especially happy ones for Casey Stengel. Though it was obvious to everyone else that the Yankees were going to win the American League pennant, the old manager was irritated by their failure to steamroller the White Sox, their only competition in a weak league. Every time the Yankees seemed about to move off by themselves, their attack sputtered and the White Sox struggled back within striking distance.

The inevitable leg trouble had hobbled Mantle, and a back injury had struck down Skowron. Both needed a rest. Many writers felt that the team, with its comfortable lead and the depth of its bench, could win without the injured players. Casey, habitually terrified at the prospect of having victory snatched away from him at the last moment, pressed them back into service. They were of little use, but the Yankees finally clinched the pennant on September 23. Having aggravated their injuries, neither player could help the team in the World Series.

Writers who were tempted to criticize Stengel restrained themselves because they were aware of his position at the Stadium. The Yankee owners demand victory *today*. Stengel believed he needed his two power hitters in the lineup to stave off the White

Sox, and in the face of the owners' demands he decided to hold nothing back for the next day in his final drive for the pennant.

Perhaps Casey's eagerness to win in the American League cost him the World Series. It is more likely that he would have lost even with Mantle and Skowron healthy. The Braves had brought Milwaukee its first National League pennant, and they were a determined and well-balanced team. They had as much power as the Yankees, fine pitching, and a good defense. In the opening game at the Stadium, however, they seemed paralyzed to find themselves in such surroundings with so much at stake, and were an easy mark for Whitey Ford. The Braves lost the first game, 3-1.

It was but a momentary lapse, and Stengel's dreams of an easy victory faded quickly. The Braves won the second game, 4-2, behind Lew Burdette, and the two teams packed and headed for Milwaukee. There Casey ran afoul of Wisconsin's fanatical citizens. A delegation was waiting to greet them at the little town of Sturtivant, near Milwaukee, where the Yankees were to be quartered. Nobody had told Casey that the team was to disembark there. He kept his players on the train, planning to let them work out that day at the ball park in Milwaukee. The reception committee, a horde of excited townsfolk and a high school band were left standing on the Sturtivant station platform.

The jilted delegation was understandably furious. Casey, unaware of the plans, had a legitimate excuse in the face of their wrath. However, he and his players had no excuse for brushing off a hastily organized welcoming committee at the Milwaukee station. Then, rubbing salt into the wounds of the indignant Milwaukeeans, a minor team official was heard to remark that he considered the fans' enthusiasm "bush league."

Casey was a most unpopular man in Milwaukee. Every time he appeared on the field to talk to one of his pitchers he was assailed by a deafening wave of hoots and boos. Then, walking back to the dugout under one such barrage, he lingered for a moment on the top step of the dugout, looked up at the fans and, just before disappearing, gallantly blew them a kiss.

The venom was gone from their hoots. A police escort, assigned to him for the obvious purpose of staving off enraged burghers intent on tearing him to pieces and pouring his blood down the sewers, found itself performing the far less glamorous task of defending Casey against enthusiastic autograph hunters. The fans still hurled insults at him but, for the most part, they were good-natured jibes. By then they wished him a fate no worse than defeat at the hands of their heroes.

The Yankees silenced them for a moment as they slaughtered their heroes, 12-3, in the third game of the Series, and gave them a nasty turn the next day by battling back to wipe out a three-run Milwaukee lead with two out in the ninth inning. Adding another run in the tenth, the Yankees led, 5-4, as the Braves came to bat in the bottom of that inning. Johnny Logan drove in a run with a double and the score was tied once again. That brought Ed Mathews, the Braves' lefthanded home run hitter, to the plate, to bat against Bob Grim. With first base open, Stengel could have ordered Grim to walk Mathews and pitch to the righthand-hitting Hank Aaron. Instead, Casey let Grim pitch to Mathews. Eddie hit a home run and the Braves won the fourth game.

"I still think I was right," Casey said later. "All they needed was a single to win, and Aaron was a better bet to get a hit than the other fella. Anyway, we'd been having pretty good luck with Mathews."

As the team was driven in a chartered bus to its hotel, it ran the gauntlet of thousands of happy Milwaukee fans who swarmed through the streets of the city. Casey, sitting at a window in the front of the bus, must have felt like a captured enemy chieftain being led through Rome. It was an unpredictable crowd. It screamed insults at him from the sidewalks, and taunted him with cries of "Busher!" Then, when the bus had stopped for a red light, many of them rushed it and besieged Casey for his autograph. Programs, photographs, scraps of paper and anything which could conceivably be signed were thrust through the window. He signed everything handed him. "Give 'em here," he said. "I'll sign anything but veal cutlets. My ball point pen slips on cutlets."

When the bus had moved on, a man sitting next to Casey asked, "How can you do that after losing a tough ball game and taking that abuse?"

Casey shrugged. "You gotta lose sometime," he said, "and when you do, lose 'em right."

New York lost the Series "right." Burdette shut out the Yankees in the fifth game, and when the teams returned to New York, Milwaukee needed only one

191

more victory. The Yankees hung on for a day, winning the sixth game, but Burdette came back to shut them out, 5-0, in the seventh game.

The Braves' clubhouse was a scene of wild disorder. They had brought Milwaukee its first championship, and had done it by beating Casey Stengel and the mighty Yankees. The celebration was in full blast when the door opened and the manager of the Yankees walked in. He went straight to Braves manager Fred Haney and owner Lou Perini, the man who had fired him years before in Boston. Casey stuck out his hand, grinned and said, "You fellas done splendid."

*   *   *   *

Stengel's string of pennants and world championships has not diminished his hunger for victory. There are many fans, writers and baseball men who believe he is the greatest manager the game has had. Casey would like to retire with that acclaim, and he knows that by surpassing Joe McCarthy's record of seven World Series triumphs he will take a giant step toward its realization. Had the Yankees beaten the Braves in 1957, he would have tied McCarthy's mark. There will be other summers.

Perhaps Casey will really retire when he has added two more World Series victories to his already astonishing list of achievements. If he does, it will come as a surprise to Edna, for she gave up trying to coax him into retirement years ago. With resignation in her voice but pride in her eyes, she says, "Baseball needs him more than I do."

Baseball is grateful to both of the Stengels.